APPLETONS' POPULAR LIBRARY

OF THE BEST AUTHORS.

PUNCH'S PRIZE NOVELISTS—THE FAT CONTRIBUTOR—TRAVELS IN LONDON.

BOOKS BY THACKERAY.

JUST PUBLISHED IN THIS SERIES,

THE LUCK OF BARRY LYNDON: a Romance of the Last Century. 2 vols. 16mo. $1.

CONFESSIONS OF FITZ BOODLE AND MAJOR GAHAGAN. 1 vol. 16mo. 50 cents.

MEN'S WIVES. 1 vol. 16mo. 50 cents.

A SHABBY GENTEEL STORY, AND OTHER TALES. 1 vol. 16mo. 50 cents.

A LEGEND OF THE RHINE; REBECCA AND ROWENA, and other Tales (*just ready*). 1 vol. 16mo. 50 cents.

THE BOOK OF SNOBS. 1 vol. 16mo. 50 cents.

THE PARIS SKETCH BOOK. 2 vols. 16mo. $1.

THE YELLOWPLUSH PAPERS. 1 vol. 16mo. 50 cents.

PUNCH'S PRIZE NOVELISTS,

THE FAT CONTRIBUTOR,

AND

TRAVELS IN LONDON.

BY

W. M. THACKERAY,

AUTHOR OF "VANITY FAIR," "MR. BROWN'S LETTERS TO A YOUNG MAN ABOUT TOWN," ETC.

NEW-YORK:
D. APPLETON & COMPANY, 200 BROADWAY.
1853.

CONTENTS.

PUNCH'S PRIZE NOVELISTS.

PUNCH'S PRIZE NOVELISTS.

PUNCH'S PRIZE NOVELISTS—so called because a TWENTY THOUSAND GUINEA PRIZE is to be awarded to the successful candidate—will embrace works by some of the most celebrated authors this country boasts of.

Their tales will appear in succession, and pretty continuously, in the pages of this Miscellany.

The publication will probably occupy about five-and-thirty years, or more or less, according to the reception with which the novels meet from our enlightened patrons—the generous British people.

All novels cannot be given entire, as a century would scarcely suffice, so numerous are our authors, so prolific and so eager has been the rush with stories, when our (confidential) announcement was sent into the literary world. But fair specimens of the authors' talents will be laid before the public, illustrated in our usual style of gorgeous splendour.

The first prize will be 20,000 guineas, viz., a lottery ticket to that amount, entitling the holder to the above sum or a palace at Vienna. The second prize will be the volume of *Punch* for the current half-year. The third a subscription to the British and Foreign Institute, &c., &c.

With a pride and gratification we cannot conceal, we at once introduce the public to GEORGE DE BARNWELL, by SIR E. L. B. L., BART.

We are not at liberty to reveal the gifted author's name, but the admirers of his works will no doubt recognize, in the splendid length of the words, the frequent employment of the Beautiful and the Ideal, the brilliant display of capitals, the profuse and profound classical learning, and, above all, in the announcement that this is to be the last of his works—one who has delighted us for many years.

GEORGE DE BARNWELL.

IN the Morning of Life the Truthful wooed the Beautiful, and their offspring was Love. Like his Divine parents, He is eternal. He has his Mother's ravishing smile; his Father's steadfast eyes. He rises every day, fresh and glorious as the untired Sun-God. He is EROS, the ever young. Dark, dark were this world of ours had either Divinity left it—dark without the day-beams of the Latonian Chariotecr, darker yet without the dædal Smile of the God of the Other Bow! Dost know him, Reader?

Old is he, EROS, the ever young! He and Time were children together. CHRONES shall die, too; but Love is imperishable. Brightest of the Divinities, where has thou not been sung? Other worships pass away; the idols for whom pyramids were raised lie in the desert crumbling and almost nameless; the Olympians are fled, their fanes no longer rise among the quivering olive groves of Ilissus, or crown the emerald islets of the amethyst Ægean! These are gone, but thou remainest. There is still a garland for thy temple, a heifer for thy stone. A heifer? Ah, many a darker sacrifice. Other blood is shed at thy altars, Remorseless One, and the Poet Priest who ministers at thy Shrine draws his auguries from the bleeding hearts of men!

While Love hath no end, Can the Bard ever cease singing? In Kingly and Heroic ages, 'twas of Kings and Heroes that the Poet spake. But in these, our times, the Artisan hath his voice as well as the Monarch. The People To-Day is King, and we chronicle his woes, as They of old did the sacrifice of the princely IPHIGENIA, or the fate of the crowned AGAMEMNON.

Is ODYSSEUS less august in his rags than in his purple? Fate, Passion, Mystery, the Victim, the Avenger, the Hate that arms, the Furies that tear, the Love that bleeds, are not these with us Still? are not these still the weapons of the Artist? the colours of his pallette, the chords of his lyre? Listen! I tell thee a tale—not of Kings—but of Men—not of Thrones, but of Love, and Grief, and Crime. Listen, and but once more. 'Tis for the last time (probably) these fingers shall sweep the strings.

E. L. B. L.

NOONDAY IN CHEPE.

'Twas noonday in Chepe. High Tide in the mighty River City!—its banks well nigh overflowing with the myriad-waved Stream of Man! The toppling wains, bearing the produce of a thousand marts; the gilded equipage of the Millionary; the humbler, but yet larger, vehicle from the green metropolitan suburbs (the Hanging Gardens of our Babylon), in which every traveller might, for a modest remuneration, take a republican seat; the mercenary caroche, with its private freight; the brisk curricle of the letter-carrier, robed in royal scarlet; these and a thousand others were labouring and pressing onward, and locked and bound and hustling together in the narrow channel of Chepe. The imprecations of the charioteers were terrible. From the noble's broidered hammer-cloth, or the driving-seat of the common coach. each driver assailed the other with floods of ribald satire. The pavid matron within the one vehicle (speeding to the Bank for her semestrial pittance) shrieked and trembled; the angry DIVES hastening to his offices (to add another thousand to his heap), thrust his head over the blazoned panels, and displayed an eloquence of objurgation which his very Menials could not equal; the dauntless street urchins, as they gaily threaded the Labyrinth of Life, enjoyed the perplexities and quarrels of the scene, and exacerbated the already furious combatants by their poignant infantile satire. And the Philosopher, as he regarded the hot strife and struggle of these Candidates in the race for Gold, thought with a sigh of the Truthful and the Beautiful, and walked on, melancholy and serene.

'Twas noon in Chepe. The ware-rooms were thronged. The flaunting windows of the mercers attracted many a purchaser: the glittering panes, behind which Birmingham had glazed its simulated silver, induced rustics to pause: although only noon, the savory odours of the Cook Shops tempted the ever hungry citizen to the bun of Bath, or to the fragrant potage that mocks the turtle's flavour—the turtle! *O dapibus supremi grata testudo Jovis!* I am an Alderman when I think of thee! Well: it was noon in Chepe.

But were all battling for gain there? Among the many brilliant shops whose casements shone upon

Chepe, there stood one a century back (about which period our tale opens) devoted to the sale of Colonial produce. A rudely carved image of a negro with a fantastic plume and apron of variegated feathers, decorated the lintel. The East and the West had sent their contributions to replenish the window.

The poor slave had toiled, died perhaps, to produce yon pyramid of swarthy sugar marked "ONLY 6½*d.*"—That catty box, on which was the epigraph STRONG FAMILY CONGO ONLY 3*s.* 9*d.*, was from the country of Confutzee—That heap of dark produce bore the legend "TRY OUR REAL NUT"—'Twas Cocoa—and that nut the Cocoa-nut, whose milk has refreshed the traveller and perplexed the natural philosopher. The shop in question was, in a word, a Grocer's.

In the midst of the shop and its gorgeous contents sat one who, to judge from his appearance (though 'twas a difficult task, as, in sooth, his back was turned), had just reached that happy period of life when the Boy is expanding into the Man. O Youth, Youth! Happy and Beautiful! O fresh and roseate dawn of life; when the dew yet lies on the flowers, ere they have been scorched and withered by Passion's fiery Sun! Immersed in thought or study, and indifferent to the din around him, sate the Boy. A careless guardian was he of the treasures confided to him. The crowd passed in Chepe; he never marked it. The sun shone on Chepe; he only asked that it should illumine the page he read. The knave might filch his treasures, he was heedless of the knave. The customer might enter; but his book was all in all to him.

And indeed a customer *was* there; a little hand was tapping on the counter with a pretty impatience; a pair of arch eyes were gazing at the Boy, admiring, perhaps, his manly proportions through the homely and tightened garments he wore.

"Ahem! Sir! I say, young man!" the customer exclaimed.

"*Ton d'apameibomenos prosephe*," read on the Student, his voice choked with emotion. "What language!" he said; "How rich, how noble, how sonorous! *prosephe podas*—"

The customer burst out into a fit of laughter so shrill and cheery, that the young Student could not but turn round, and, blushing, for the first time remarked her. "A pretty Grocer's boy you are," she cried, "with your applepiebomenos and your French and lingo. Am I to be kept waiting for hever?"

"Pardon, fair Maiden," said he, with high-bred courtesy; "'Twas not French I read, 'twas the Godlike language of the blind old bard. In what can I be serviceable to ye, lady?" and to spring from his desk, to smooth his apron, to stand before her the obedient Shop Boy, the Poet no more, was the work of a moment.

I might have prigged this box of figs," the damsel said, good naturedly, "and you'd never have turned round."

"They came from the country of HECTOR," the boy said. "Would you have currants, lady? These once bloomed in the island gardens of the blue Ægean. They are uncommon fine ones, and the figure is low; they're fourpence-halfpenny a pound. Would ye mayhap make trial of our teas? We do not advertise, as some folks do: but sell as low as any other house."

"You're precious young to have all these good things," the girl exclaimed, not unwilling, seemingly, to prolong the conversation. "If I was you, and stood behind the counter, I should be eating figs the whole day long."

"Time was," answered the lad, and not long since I thought so, too, "I thought I never should be tired of figs. But my old uncle bade me take my fill, and now in sooth I am aweary of them."

"I think you gentlemen are always so," the coquette said.

"Nay, say not so, fair stranger!" the youth replied, his face kindling as he spoke, and his eagle eyes flashing fire. "Figs pall; but O! the Beautiful never does! Figs rot; but O! the Truthful is eternal. I was born, lady, to grapple with the Lofty and the Ideal. My soul yearns for the Visionary. I stand behind the counter, it is true; but I ponder here upon the deeds of heroes, and muse over the thoughts of sages. What is grocery for one who has ambition? What sweetness hath Muscovado to him who hath tasted of Poesy? The Ideal, lady, I often think, is the true Real, and the Actual but a visionary hallucination. But pardon me; with what may I serve thee?"

"I came only for sixpenn'orth of tea-dust," the girl said, with a faltering voice; "but O, I should like to hear you speak on for ever!"

Only for sixpenn'orth of tea-dust? Girl, thou camest for other things! Thou lovedst his voice? Syren! what was the witchery of thine own? He deftly made up the packet, and placed it in the little hand. She paid for her small purchase, and, with a farewell glance of her lustrous eyes, she left him. She passed slowly through the portal, and in a moment more was lost in the crowd. It was noon in Chepe. And George de Barnwell was alone.

GEORGE DE BARNWELL.—VOL. II.

BY SIR E. L. B. L. B B. L L. B B B. L L L., BART.

We have selected the following episodical chapter in preference to any relating to the mere story of George Barnwell, with which most readers are familiar.

Up to this passage (extracted from the beginning of Vol. ii.) the tale is briefly thus:—

That rogue of a Millwood has come back every day to the grocer's shop in Chepe, wanting some sugar, or some nutmeg, or some figs, half-a-dozen times in the week.

She and George de Barnwell have vowed to each other an eternal attachment.

This flame acts violently upon George. His bosom swells with ambition. His genius breaks out prodigiously. He talks about the Good, the Beautiful, the Ideal, &c., in and out of all season, and is virtuous and eloquent almost beyond belief—in fact like Devereux, or P. Clifford, or E. Aram, Esquires.

Inspired by MILLWOOD & LOVE, GEORGE robs the till, and mingles in the world which he is destined to ornament. He outdoes all the dandies, all the wits, all the scholars, and all the voluptuaries of the age—an indefinite period of time between QUEEN ANN and GEORGE II.—dines with CURLL at St. John's gate, pinks COLONEL CHARTERIS in a duel behind Montague House, is initiated into the intrigues of the CHEVALIER ST. GEORGE, whom he entertains at his sumptuous pavillion at Hampstead, and likewise in disguise at the shop in Cheapside.

His uncle, the owner of the shop, a surly curmudgeon with very little taste for the True and the Beautiful, has retired from business to the pastoral village in Cambridgeshire from which the noble BARNWELLS came. GEORGE'S cousin ANNABEL is, of course, consumed with a secret passion for him.

Some trifling inaccuracies may be remarked in the ensuing brilliant little chapter; but it must be remembered that the author wished to present an age at a glance; and the dialogue is quite as fine and correct as that in the "Last of the Barons," or in "Eugene Aram," or other works of our author, in which Sentiment and History, or the True and the Beautiful, are united.

CHAP. XXIV.

BUTTON'S IN PALL MALL.

THOSE who frequent the dismal and enormous Mansions of Silence which society has raised to Ennui in that Omphalos of town, Pall Mall, and which, because they knock you down with their dullness, are called Clubs no doubt; those who yawn from a bay-window in St. James's Street, at a half-score of other dandies gaping from another bay-window over the way; those who consult a dreary evening paper for news, or satisfy themselves with the jokes of the miserable *Punch*, by way of wit; the men about town of the present day, in a word, can have but little idea of London some six or eight score years back. Thou pudding-sided old dandy of St. James's Street, with thy lackered boots, thy dyed whiskers, and thy suffocating waistband, what art thou to thy brilliant predecessor in the same quarter? The Brougham from which thou descendest at the portal of the Carlton or the Travellers', is like every body else's; thy black coat has no more plaits, nor buttons, nor fancy in it than thy neighbour's; thy hat was made on the very block on which LORD ADDLEPATE'S was cast, who has just entered the Club before thee. You and he yawn together out of the same omnibus-box every night; you fancy yourselves men of pleasure; you fancy yourselves men of fashion; you fancy yourselves men of taste; in fancy, in taste, in opinion, in philosophy, the newspaper legislates for you; it is there you get your jokes, and your thoughts, and your facts and your wisdom—poor Pall Mall dullards. Stupid slaves of the press, on that ground which you at present occupy, there were men of wit and pleasure and fashion, some five-and-twenty lustres ago.

We are at BUTTON'S—the well-known sign of the Turk's Head. The crowd of periwigged heads at the windows—the swearing chairman round the steps (the blazoned and coronalled panels of whose vehicles denote the lofty rank of their owners),—the throng of embroidered beaux entering or departing, and rendering the air fragrant with the odours of pulvillio and pomander, proclaim the celebrated resort of London's Wit and Fashion. It is the corner of Regent Street. Carlton House has not yet been taken down.

A stately gentleman in crimson velvet and gold is sipping chocolate at one of the tables, in earnest converse with a friend whose suit is likewise embroidered, but stained by time, or wine mayhap, or wear. A little deformed gentleman in iron-gray is reading the *Morning Chronicle* newspaper by the fire, while a divine, with a broad brogue and a shovel hat and cassock is talking freely with a gentleman, whose star and riband, as well as the unmistakeable beauty of his Phidian countenance, proclaims him to be a member of Britain's aristocracy.

Two ragged youths, the one tall, gaunt, clumsy and scrofulous; the other with a wild, careless, beautiful look, evidently indicating Race, are gazing in at the window, not merely at the crowd in the celebrated Club, but at TIMOTHY, the waiter, who is removing a plate of that exquisite dish, the muffin (then newly invented), at the desire of some of the revellers within.

"I would, SAM," said the wild youth to his companion, "that I had some of my Mother MACCLESFIELD's gold, to enable us to eat of those cates and mingle with yon springalds and beaux."

"To vaunt a knowledge of the stoical philosophy," said the youth addressed as SAM, "might elicit a smile of incredulity upon the cheek of the parasite of pleasure; but there are moments in life when History fortifies endurance: and past study renders present deprivation more bearable. If our pecuniary resources be exiguous, let our resolution, DICK, supply the deficiencies of Fortune. The muffin we desire to-day would little benefit us to-morrow. Poor and hungry, as we are, are we less happy, DICK, than yon listless voluptuary who banquets on the food which you covet?"

And the two lads turned away up Waterloo Place, and past the Parthenon Club-house, and disappeared to take a meal of cow-heel at a neighbouring cook's shop. Their names were SAMUEL JOHNSON and RICHARD SAVAGE.

Meanwhile the conversation at BUTTON'S was fast and brilliant. "By WOOD'S thirteens, and the divvle go wid 'em," cried the Church dignitary in the cassock, "is it in blue and goold ye are this morning, SIR RICHARD, when you ought to be in seebles?"

"Who's dead, DEAN?" said the nobleman, the dean's companion.

"Faix, mee LARD BOLINGBROKE, as sure as mee name's JONATHAN SWIFT—and I'm not so sure of that neither, for who knows his father's name?—there's been a mighty cruel murther committed entirely. A child of DICK STEELE'S has been barbarously slain, dthrawn, and quarthered, and it's JOE ADDISON yondther has done it. Ye should have killed one of your own, JOE, ye thief of the world."

"I!" said the amazed and RIGHT HONOURABLE JOSEPH ADDISON; "I kill DICK'S child! I was Godfather to the last."

"And promised a cup and never sent it," DICK ejaculated. JOSEPH looked grave.

"The child I mean is SIR ROGER DE COVERLEY, KNIGHT AND BARONET. What made ye kill him, ye savage Mohock? The whole town is in tears about the good knight; all the ladies at Church this afternoon were in mourning; all the booksellers are wild;

and LINTOT says not a third of the copies of the *Spectator* are sold since the death of the brave old gentleman." And the DEAN OF ST. PATRICK'S pulled out the *Spectator* newspaper, containing the well-known passage regarding SIR ROGER'S death. "I bought it but now in "Wellington-street," he said; "the news-boys were howling all down the Strand."

"What a miracle is Genius—Genius, the Divine and Beautiful," said a gentleman leaning against the same fire-place with the deformed cavalier in iron-grey, and addressing that individual, who was in fact MR. ALEXANDER POPE, "what a marvellous gift is this, and royal privilege of Art! To make the Ideal more credible than the Actual: to enchain our hearts, to command our hopes, our regrets, our tears, for a mere brain-born Emanation: to invest with life the Incorporeal, and to glamour the cloudy into substance,—these are the lofty privileges of the Poet, if I have read poesy aright; and I am as familiar with the sounds that rang from HOMER'S lyre, as with the strains which celebrate the loss of BELINDA'S lovely locks, (MR. POPE blushed and bowed, highly delighted)—"these, I say, sir, are the privileges of the Poet—the Poietes—the Maker—he moves the world, and asks no lever; if he cannot charm death into life as ORPHEUS feigned to do, he can create Beauty out of Naught, and defy Death by rendering Thought Eternal. Ho! JEMMY, another flask of Nantz."

And the boy—for he who addressed the most brilliant company of wits in Europe was little more—emptied the contents of the brandy-flask into a silver flagon, and quaffed it gaily to the health of the company assembled. 'Twas the third he had taken during the sitting. Presently, and with a graceful salute to the Society, he quitted the coffee-house, and was seen entering on a magnificent Arab past the National Gallery.

"Who is yon spark in blue and silver? He beats JOE ADDISON, himself, in drinking, and pious JOE is the greatest toper in the three kingdoms," DICK STEELE said good-naturedly.

"His paper in the *Spectator* beats thy best, DICK, thou sluggard," the RIGHT HONOURABLE MR. ADDISON exclaimed. "He is the author of that famous No. 996, for which you have all been giving me the credit."

"The rascal foiled me at capping verses," DEAN SWIFT said; "and won a tenpenny piece of me, plague take him!"

"He has suggested an emendation in my 'Homer,' which proves him a delicate scholar," MR. POPE exclaimed.

"He knows more of the French king than any man I have met with; and we must have an eye upon him," said LORD BOLINGBROKE, then Secretary of State for Foreign Affairs, and beckoning a suspicious-looking person who was drinking at a side-table, whispered to him something.

Meantime who was he? where was he, this youth who had struck all the wits of London with admiration? His galloping charger had returned to the City; his splendid court-suit was doffed for the citizen's gabardine and grocer's humble apron.

George de Barnwell was in Chepe—in Chepe, at the feet of Martha Millwood.

GEORGE DE BARNWELL.—VOL III.

BY SIR E. L. B. L. B B. L L. B B B. L L L., BART.

THE CONDEMNED CELL.

"*Quid me mollibus implicas lacertis*, my ELLINOR? Nay," GEORGE added, a faint smile illumining his wan but noble features, "why speak to thee in the accents of the Roman poet, which thou comprehendest not? Bright One, there be other things in Life, in Nature, in this Inscrutable Labyrinth, this Heart on which thou leanest, which are equally unintelligible to thee! Yes, my pretty one, what is the Unintelligible but the Ideal? what is the Ideal but the Beautiful? what the Beautiful but the Eternal? And the Spirit of Man that would commune with these is like Him who wanders by the *thina poluphloisboio thalasses*, and shrinks awe-struck before that Azure Mystery."

EMILY's eyes filled with fresh-gushing dew. "Speak on, speak ever thus, my GEORGE," she exclaimed. BARNWELL's chains rattled as the confiding girl clung to him. Even SNOGGIN, the Turnkey appointed to sit with the Prisoner, was affected by his noble and appropriate language, and also burst into tears.

"You weep, my SNOGGIN," the Boy said; ".and why? Hath Life been so charming to me that I should wish to retain it? Hath Pleasure no after-Weariness? Ambition no Deception; Wealth no Care; and Glory no Mockery? Psha! I am sick of Success, palled of Pleasure, weary of Wine, and Wit, and—nay, start not, my ADELAIDE—and Woman. I fling away all these things as the Toys of Boyhood. Life is the Soul's Nursery. I am a Man, and pine for the Illimitable! Mark you me! Has the Morrow any terrors for me, think ye? Did SOCRATES falter at his poison? Did SENECA blench in his bath? Did BRUTUS shirk the sword when his Great Stake was lost? Did even weak CLEOPATRA shrink from the Serpent's fatal nip? and why should I? My great Hazard hath been played, and I pay my forfeit. Lie sheathed in my heart, thou flashing Blade! Welcome to my Bosom, thou faithful Serpent; I hug thee, peace-bearing Image of the Eternal! Ha, the hemlock cup! Fill high, boy, for my soul is thirsty for the Infinite! Get ready the bath, friends; prepare me for the feast of To-morrow—

bathe my limbs in odours, and put ointment in my hair."

"Has for a bath," SNOGGIN interposed, "they're not to be ad in this ward of the prison; but I dussay HEMMY will git you a little hoil for your air."

The Prisoned One laughed loud and merrily. "My guardian understands me not, pretty one—and thou? what sayst thou? from those dear lips methinks—*plura sunt oscula quam sententiæ*—I kiss away thy tears, dove!—they will flow apace when I am gone, then they will dry, and presently these fair eyes will shine on another, as they have beamed on poor GEORGE BARNWELL. Yet wilt thou not all forget him, sweet one. He was an honest fellow, and had a kindly heart, for all the world said—"

"That, that he had," cried the gaoler and the girl in voices gurgling with emotion. And you who read! you unconvicted Convict—you, murderer, though haply you have slain no one—you, Felon *in posse*, if not *in esse*—deal gently with one who has used the Opportunity that has failed thee—and believe that the Truthful and the Beautiful bloom sometimes in the dock and the convict's tawny Gabardine!

* * * * * * *

In the matter for which he suffered, GEORGE could never be brought to acknowledge that he was at all in the wrong. "It may be an error of judgment," he said to the Venerable Chaplain of the gaol, "but it is no crime. Were it Crime, I should feel Remorse. Where there is no Remorse, Crime cannot exist. I am not sorry: therefore, I am innocent. Is the proposition a fair one?"

The excellent Doctor admitted that it was not to be contested.

"And wherefore, Sir, should I have sorrow," the Boy resumed, "for ridding the world of a sordid worm; * of a man whose very soul was dross, and who never had a feeling for the Truthful and the Beautiful? When I stood before my uncle in the moonlight, in the gardens of the ancestral halls of the DE BARNWELLS, I felt that it was the NEMESIS come to overthrow him. 'Dog,' I said to the trembling slave, 'tell me where thy Gold is. *Thou* hast no use for it. I can spend it in relieving the Poverty on which thou tramplest; in aiding Science, which thou knowest not; in uplifting Art, to

* This is a gross plagiarism: the above sentiment is expressed much more eloquently in the ingenious romance of *Eugene Aram*:—"The burning desires I have known—the resplendent visions I have nursed—the sublime aspirings that have lifted me so often from sense and clay: these tell me, that whether for good or ill, I am the thing of an immortality, and the creature of a God. * * * * I have destroyed a man noxious to the world; with the wealth by which he afflicted society, I have been the means of blessing many."

which thou art blind. Give Gold, and thou art free.' But he spake not, and I slew him."

"I would not have this doctrine vulgarly promulgated," said the admirable chaplain, "for its general practice might chance to do harm. Thou, my son, the Refined, the Gentle, the Loving and Beloved, the Poet and Sage, urged by what I cannot but think a grievous error, hast appeared as Avenger. Think what would be the world's condition, were men without any Yearning after the Ideal to attempt to reorganise Society, to redistribute Property, to avenge Wrong."

"A rabble of pigmies scaling Heaven," said the noble, though misguided young Prisoner. "PROMETHEUS was a Giant, and he fell."

"Yes, indeed, my brave youth!" the benevolent DR. FUZZWIG exclaimed, clasping the Prisoner's marble and manacled hand; "and the Tragedy of To-morrow will teach the World that Homicide is not to be permitted even to the most amiable Genius, and that the lover of the Ideal and the Beautiful, as thou art, my son, must respect the Real likewise."

"Look! here is supper!" cried BARNWELL gaily. "This is the Real, Doctor; let us respect it and fall to." He partook of the meal as joyously as if it had been one of his early festals; but the worthy chaplain could scarcely eat it for tears.

PHIL. FOGARTY.—A Tale of the Fighting Onety-oneth.

BY HARRY ROLLICKER.

I.

The gabion was ours. After two hours' fighting we were in possession of the first embrasure, and made ourselves as comfortable as circumstances would admit. Jack Delamere, Tom Delancy, Jerry Blake, the Doctor, and myself, sate down under a pontoon, and our servants laid out a hasty supper on a tumbril. Though Cambacères had escaped me so provokingly after I cut him down, his spoils were mine; a cold fowl and a Bologna sausage were found in the Marshal's holsters; and in the haversack of a French private who lay a corpse on the glacis, we found a loaf of bread, his three days' ration. Instead of salt, we had gunpowder; and you may be sure, wherever the Doctor was, a flask of good brandy was behind him in his instrument-case. We sate down and made a soldier's supper. The Doctor pulled a few of the delicious fruit from the lemon trees growing near (and round which the Carabiniers and the 24th Leger had made a desperate rally), and punch was brewed in JACK DELAMERE's helmet.

"Faith, it never had so much wit in it before," said the Doctor, as he ladled out the drink. We all roared with laughing, except the guardsman, who was as savage as a Turk at a christening.

"*Buvez-en*" said old SAWBONES to our French prisoner; "*ça vous fera du bien, mon vieux coq!*" and the Colonel, whose wound had been just dressed, eagerly grasped at the proffered cup, and drained it with a health to the donors.

How strange are the chances of war! But half-an-hour before he and I were engaged in mortal combat, and our prisoner was all but my conqueror. Grappling with CAMBACERES, whom I had knocked from his horse, and was about to dispatch, I felt a lunge behind, which luckily was parried by my sabretache; a herculean grasp was at the next instant at my throat—I was on the ground—my prisoner had escaped, and a gigantic warrior in the uniform of a colonel of the regiment of Artois glaring over me with pointed sword.

"*Rends toi, coquin!*" said he.

"*Allez au Diable*," said I, "a FOGARTY never surrenders."

I thought of my poor mother and my sisters, at the old house in Killaloo—I felt the tip of his blade between my teeth—I breathed a prayer, and shut my eyes—when the tables were turned—the butt-end of LANTY CLANCY's musket knocked the sword up and broke the arm that held it.

"*Thonamoundiaoul nabochlish*," said the French officer, with a curse in the purest Irish. It was lucky I stopped laughing time enough to bid LANTY hold his hand, for the honest fellow would else have brained my gallant adversary. We were the better friends for our combat, as what gallant hearts are not?

The breach was to be stormed at sunset, and like true soldiers we sate down to make the most of our time. The rogue of a Doctor took the liver-wing for his share—we gave the other to our guest, a prisoner; those scoundrels TOM DELAMERE and JACK DELANCY took the legs—and, faith, poor I was put off with the Pope's-nose and a bit of the back.

"How d'ye like his Holiness's *fayture?*" said JERRY BLAKE.

"Any how you'll have a *merry thought*," cried the incorrigible Doctor, and all the party shrieked at the witticism.

"*De mortuis nil nisi bonum*," said JACK, holding up the drum-stick clean.

"Faith, there's not enough of it to make us *chicken-hearted*, anyhow," said I; "come, boys, let's have a song."

"Here goes," said TOM DELANCY, and sang the following lyric, of his own composition:—

"Dear JACK, this white mug that with GUINNESS I fill,
And drink to the health of sweet NAN of the Hill,
Was once TOMMY TOSSPOT'S, as jovial a sot,
As e'er drew a spiggot, or drained a full pot—
In drinking, all round 'twas his joy to surpass,
And with all merry tipplers he swigg'd off his glass.

"One morning in summer, while seated so snug,
In the porch of his garden, discussing his jug,
Stern Death, on a sudden, to TOM did appear,
And said 'Honest THOMAS, come take your last bier;'
We kneaded his clay in the shape of this can,
From which let us drink to the health of my NAN."

"Psha!" said the Doctor, "I've heard that song before; here's a new one for you, boys!" and SAWBONES began, in a rich Corkagian voice—

"You've all heard of LARRY O'TOOLE,
Of the beautiful town of Drumgoole;
He had but one eye,
To ogle ye by—
O, murther, but that was a jew'l!
A fool
He made of de girls, dis O'TOOLE.

"'Twas he was the boy didn't fail,
That tuck down pataties and mail;
He never would shrink
From any sthrong dthrink,

Was it whisky or Drogheda ale;
I'm bail
This LARRY would swallow a pail.

"O, many a night, at the bowl,
With LARRY I've sot cheek by jowl;
He's gone to his rest,
Where there's dthrink of the best,
And so let us give his old sowl
A howl,
For 'twas he made the noggin to rowl."

I observed the French Colonel's eye glisten, as he heard these well-known accents of his country; but we were too well-bred to pretend to remark his emotion.

The sun was setting behind the mountains as our songs were finished, and each began to look out with some anxiety for the preconcerted signal, the rocket from SIR HUSSEY VIVIAN'S quarters, which was to announce the recommencement of hostilities It came just as the moon rose in her silver splendour, and ere the rocket-stick fell quivering to the earth at the feet of GENERAL PICTON and SIR LOWRY COLE, who were at their posts at the head of the storming parties, nine hundred-and-ninety-nine guns in position opened their fire from our batteries, which were answered by a tremendous cannonnade from the fort.

"Who's going to dance," said the Doctor, "the ball's begun. Ha! there goes poor JACK DELAMERE'S head off! The ball chose a soft one, any how. Come here, Tim, till I mend your leg. Your wife has need only knit half as many stockings next year, Doolan, my boy. Faix! there goes a big one had well nigh stopped my talking; bedad! it has snuffed the feather off my cocked hat!"

In this way, with eighty-four pounders roaring over us like hail, the undaunted little doctor pursued his jokes and his duty. That he had a feeling heart, all who served with him knew, and none more so than Philip Fogarty, the humble writer of this tale of war.

Our embrasure was luckily bomb-proof, and the detachment of the gallant Onety-oneth under my orders, suffered comparatively little. "Be cool, boys," I said; "it will be hot enough work for you ere long." The honest fellows answered with an Irish cheer. I saw that it affected our prisoner.

"Countryman," said I, "I know you; but an Irishman was never a traitor."

"*Taisez-vous!*" said he, putting his finger to his lip. "*C'est la fortune de la guerre:* if ever you come to Paris, ask for the Marquis d' O'Mahony, and I may render you the hospitality which your tyrannous laws prevent me from exercising in the ancestral halls of my own race."

I shook him warmly by the hand as a tear bedimmed his eye. It was, then, the celebrated colonel of the Irish Brigade created a Marquis by Napoleon on the field of Austerlitz!

"Marquis," said I, "the country which disowns you is proud of you; but—ha! here, if I mistake not, comes our signal to advance." And in fact Captain Vandeleur, riding up through the shower of shot, asked for the commander of the detachment, and bade me hold myself in readiness to move as soon as the flank companies of the Ninety-ninth, and Sixty-sixth, and the Grenadier Brigade of the German Legion began to advance up the echelon. The devoted band soon arrived; Jack Bowser heading the Ninety-ninth, (when was he away and a storming party to the fore?), and the gallant Potztausend with his Hanoverian veterans.

The second rocket flew up.

"Forward, Onety-oneth!" cried I, in a voice of thunder. "Killaloo boys, follow your captain!" and with a shrill hurray, that sounded above the tremendous fire from the fort, we sprung up the steep; Bowser, with the brave Ninety-ninth, and the bold Potztausend, keeping well up with us. We passed the demilune, we passed the culverin, bayonetting the artillery-men at their guns; we advanced across the two tremendous demilunes which flank the counterscarp, and prepared for the final spring upon the citadel. Soult I could see quite pale on the wall; and the scoundrel Cambacères, who had been so nearly my prisoner that day, trembled as he cheered his men. "On boys, on!" I hoarsely exclaimed. "Hurroo," said the fighting Onety-oneth.

But there was a movement among the enemy. An officer, glittering with orders, and another in a grey coat and a cocked hat, came to the wall, and I recognised the EMPEROR NAPOLEON and the famous JOACHIM MURAT.

"We are hardly pressed, methinks," NAPOLEON said, sternly. "I must exercise my old trade as an artillery-man;" and MURAT loaded, and the EMPEROR pointed the only hundred-and-twenty-four pounder that had not been silenced by our fire.

"Hurray, Killaloo boys!" shouted I. The next moment a sensation of numbness and death seized me, and I lay like a corpse upon the rampart.

II.

"HUSH!" said a voice, which I recognised to be that of the MARQUIS DE MAHONY. "Heaven be praised, reason has returned to you. For six weeks those are the only sane words I have heard from you."

"Faix, and 'tis thrue for you, Colonel dear," cried another voice, with which I was even more familiar; 'twas that of my honest and gallant LANTY CLANCY, who was blubbering at my bedside, overjoyed at his master's recovery.

"O musha! MASTHER PHIL. Agrah! but this will be the great day intirely, when I send off the news, which I would, barrin' I can't write, to the lady, your mother, and your sisters, at Castle Fogarty; and 'tis his Riv'rence FATHER LUKE will jump for joy thin, when he reads the letthur! Six weeks ravin' and roarin' as bould as a lion, and as mad as MICK MALONY'S pig, that mistuck MICK'S wig for a cabbage, and died of atin' it!"

"And have I then lost my senses?" I exclaimed feebly.

"Sure, didn't ye call me your beautiful DONNA ANNA only yesterday, and catch hould of me whiskers as if they were the Signora's jet black ringlets?" LANTY cried.

At this moment, and blushing deeply, the most beautiful young creature I ever set my eyes upon, rose from a chair at the foot of the bed, and sailed out of the room.

"Confusion! you blundering rogue," I cried, "who is that lovely lady whom you frightened away by your impertinence. DONNA ANNA? Where am I?"

"You are in good hands, PHILIP," said the Colonel; "you are at my house in the Place Vendôme, at Paris, of which I am the Military Governor. You and LANTY were knocked down by the wind of the cannon-ball at Burgos. Do not be ashamed: 'twas the EMPEROR pointed the gun;" and the Colonel took off his hat as he mentioned the name darling to France. "When our troops returned from the sally in which your gallant storming party was driven back, you were found on the glacis, and I had you brought into the city. Your reason had left you, however, when you returned to life; but, unwilling to desert the son of my old friend, PHILIP FOGARTY, who saved my life in '98, I brought you in my carriage to Paris."

"And many's the time you tried to jump out of the windy, MASTHER PHIL," said CLANCY.

"Brought you to Paris," resumed the Colonel, smiling; "where, by the *soins* of my friends BROUSSAIS, ESQUIROL, and BARON LARREY, you have been restored to health, thank Heaven!"

"And that lovely angel who quitted the apartment?" I cried.

"That lovely angel is the LADY BLANCHE SARSFIELD, my ward, a descendant of the gallant LUCAN, and who may be, when she chooses, MADAME LA MARÉCHALE DE CAMBACÈRES, DUCHESS OF ILLYRIA."

"Why did you deliver the ruffian when he was in my grasp?" I cried.

"Why did LANTY deliver you when in mine?" the Colonel replied. "*C'est la fortune de la guerre, mon garçon;* but calm yourself, and take this potion which BLANCHE has prepared for you."

I drank the *tisane* eagerly when I heard whose

fair hands had compounded it, and its effects were speedily beneficial to me, for I sank into a cool and refreshing slumber.

From that day I began to mend rapidly, with all the elasticity of youth's happy time. BLANCHE—the enchanting BLANCHE—ministered henceforth to me, for I would take no medicine but from her lily hand. And what were the effects? Faith, ere a month was past, the patient was over head and ears in love with the doctor; and as for BARON LARREY, and BROUSSAIS, and ESQUIROL, they were sent to the right-about. In a short time I was in a situation to do justice to the *gigot aux navets*, the *bœuf aux cornichons*, and the other delicious *entremets* of the Marquis's board, with an appetite that astonished some of the Frenchmen who frequented it.

"Wait till he's quite well, Miss," said LANTY, who waited always behind me. "Faith! when he's in health, I'd back him to ate a cow, barrin' the horns and teel." I sent a decanter at the rogue's head, by way of answer to his impertinence.

Although the disgusting CAMBACÈRES did his best to have my parole withdrawn from me, and to cause me to be sent to the English depôt of prisoners at Verdun, the Marquis's interest with the EMPEROR prevailed, and I was allowed to remain at Paris, the happiest of prisoners at the Colonel's hotel at the Place Vendôme. I here had the opportunity (an opportunity not lost, I flatter myself, on a young fellow with the accomplishments of PHILIP FOGARTY, ESQ.) of mixing with the *élite* of French society, and meeting with many of the great, the beautiful, and the brave. TALLEYRAND was a frequent guest of the Marquis's. His *bon-mots* used to keep the table in a roar. NEY frequently took his chop with us; MURAT, when in town, constantly dropt in for a cup of tea and friendly round game. Alas! who would have thought those two gallant heads would be so soon laid low? My wife has a pair of ear-rings which the latter, who always wore them, presented to her—but we are advancing matters. Anybody could see, "*avec un demi-œil*," as the PRINCE OF BENEVENT remarked, how affairs went between me and BLANCHE; but though she loathed him for his cruelties and the odiousness of his person, the brutal CAMBACÈRES still pursued his designs upon her.

I recollect, it was on ST. PATRICK's Day. My lovely friend had procured, from the gardens of the EMPRESS JOSEPHINE, at Malmaison, (whom we loved a thousand times more than her Austrian successor, a sandy-haired woman, between ourselves, with an odious squint,) a quantity of shamrock wherewith to garnish the hotel, and all the Irish in Paris were invited to the national festival.

I and PRINCE TALLEYRAND danced a double hornpipe with PAULINE BONAPARTE and MADAME DE

STAEL; MARSHAL SOULT went down a couple of sets with MADAME RECAMIER; and ROBESPIERRE'S widow —an excellent, gentle creature, quite unlike her husband—stood up with the AUSTRIAN AMBASSADOR. Besides, the famous artists BARON GROS, DAVID and NICHOLAS POUSSIN, and CANOVA, who was in town making a statue of the Emperor, for LEO X., and in a word all the celebrities of Paris—as my gifted countrywoman, the wild Irish girl, calls them—were assembled in the Marquis's elegant receiving-rooms.

At last a great outcry was raised for *La Gigue Irlandaise! La Gigue Irlandaise!* a dance which had made *fureur* amongst the Parisians ever since the lovely BLANCHE SARSFIELD had danced it. She stepped forward and took me for a partner, and amidst the bravos of the crowd, in which stood NEY, MURAT, LANNES, the PRINCE OF WAGRAM, and the AUSTRIAN AMBASSADOR, we showed to the *beau monde* of the French capital, I flatter myself, a not unfavourable specimen of the dance of our country.

As I was cutting the double-shuffle, and toe-and-heeling it in the "rail" style, BLANCHE danced up to me, smiling, and said, "Be on your guard; I see CAMBACÈRES talking to FOUCHÉ the Duke of Otranto about us—and when OTRANTO turns his eyes upon a man, they bode him no good."

"CAMBACÈRES is jealous," said I. "I have it," says she; "I'll make him dance a turn with me."

So presently, as the music was going like mad all this time, I pretended fatigue from my late wounds, and sate down The lovely BLANCHE went up smiling, and brought out CAMBACÈRES as a second partner.

The Marshal is a lusty man, who makes desperate efforts to give himself a waist, and the effect of the exercise upon him was speedily visible. He puffed and snorted like a walrus, drops trickled down his purple face, while my lovely mischief of a BLANCHE went on dancing at treble quick, till she fairly danced him down.

"Who 'll take the flure with me?" said the charming girl, animated by the sport.

"Faix, den, 'tis I, LANTY CLANCY!" cried my rascal, who had been mad with excitement at the scene; and, stepping in with a whoop and a hurroo, he began to dance with such a rapidity as made all present stare.

As the couple were footing it, there was a noise as of a rapid cavalcade traversing the Place Vendôme, and stopping at the Marquis's door. A crowd appeared to mount the stair; the great doors of the reception-room were flung open, and two pages announced their Majesties the Emperor and the Empress. So engaged were LANTY and BLANCHE, that they never heard the tumult occasioned by the august approach.

It was indeed the Emperor who, returning from the Théâtre Français, and seeing the Marquis's windows lighted up, proposed to the Empress to drop in on the party. He made signs to the musicians to continue: and the conqueror of Marengo and Friedland watched with interest the simple evolutions of two happy Irish people. Even the Empress smiled; and, seeing this, all the courtiers, including NAPLES and TALLEYRAND, were delighted.

"Is not this a great day for Ireland?" said the Marquis, with a tear trickling down his noble face. "O Ireland! O my country! But no more of that. Go up, PHIL, you divvle, and offer her Majesty the choice of punch or negus."

III.

AMONG the young fellows with whom I was most intimate in Paris was EUGÈNE BEAUHARNAIS, the son of the ill-used and unhappy JOSEPHINE by her former marriage with a French gentleman of good family. Having a smack of the old blood in him, EUGÈNE's manners were much more refined than those of the new-fangled dignitaries of the EMPEROR's Court; where (for my knife and fork were regularly laid at the Tuileries) I have seen my poor friend MURAT repeatedly mistake a fork for a tooth-pick, and the gallant MASSENA devour peas by means of his knife, in a way more innocent than graceful. TALLEYRAND, EUGÈNE, and I, used often to laugh at these eccentricities of our brave friends, who certainly did not shine in the drawing-room, however brilliant they were in the field of battle. The EMPEROR always asked me to take wine with him, and was full of kindness and attention. "I like EUGÈNE" (he would say to me, pinching my ear confidentially, as his way was,) —"I like EUGÈNE to keep company with such young fellows as you; you have manners; you have principles; my rogues from the camp have none. And I like you, PHILIP, my boy," he added, "for being so attentive to my poor wife—the EMPRESS JOSEPHINE, I mean." All these honours made my friends at the Marquis's very proud, and my enemies at Court *crêver* with envy. Among these, the atrocious CAMBACÈRES was not the least active and envenomed.

The cause of the many attentions which were paid to me, and which like a vain coxcomb, I had chosen to attribute to my own personal amiability, soon was apparent. Having formed a good opinion of my gallantry from my conduct in various actions and forlorn hopes during the war, the EMPEROR was most anxious to attach me to his service. The grand Cross of St. Louis, the title of Count, the command of a crack cavalry regiment, the 14me Chevaux Marins, were the bribes that were actually offered to me; and, must I say it! BLANCHE, the lovely, the perfidious BLANCHE, was one of the agents employed to tempt me to commit this act of treason.

"Object to enter a foreign service!" she said, in reply to my refusal. "It is you, PHILIP, who are in a foreign service. The Irish nation is in exile, and in the territories of its French allies. Irish traitors are not here; they march alone under the accursed flag of the Saxon, whom the great NAPOLEON would have swept from the face of the earth, but for the fatal valour of Irish mercenaries! Accept this offer, and my heart, my hand, my all are yours. Refuse it, PHILIP, and we part."

"To wed the abominable CAMBACÈRES!" I cried, stung with rage. "To wear a duchess's coronet, BLANCHE! Ha, ha! Mushrooms, instead of strawberry-leaves, should decorate the brows of the upstart French nobility. I shall withdraw my parole. I demand to be sent to prison—to be exchanged—to die—anything rather than be a traitor, and the tool of a traitress!" Taking up my hat, I left the room in a fury; and flinging open the door, tumbled over CAMBACÈRES, who was listening at the key-hole, and must have overheard every word of our conversation.

We tumbled over each other, as BLANCHE was shrieking with laughter at our mutual discomfiture. Her scorn only made me more mad; and, having spurs on, I began digging them into CAMBACÈRES' fat sides as we rolled on the carpet, until the Marshal howled with rage and anger.

"This insult must be avenged with blood!" roared the DUKE OF ILLYRIA.

"I have already drawn it," says I, "with my spurs."

"*Malheur et malèdiction!*" roared the Marshal.

"Hadn't you better settle your wig?" says I, offering it to him on the tip of my cane, "and we'll arrange time and place when you have put your jasey in order." I shall never forget the look of revenge which he cast at me, as I was thus turning him into ridicule before his mistress.

"LADY BLANCHE," I continued bitterly, "as you look to share the Duke's coronet, hadn't you better see to his wig?" and so saying, I cocked my hat, and walked out of the Marquis's place, whistling "Garry-owen."

I knew my man would not be long in following me, and waited for him in the Place Vendôme, where I luckily met EUGÈNE too, who was looking at the picture-shop in the corner. I explained to him my affair in a twinkling. He at once agreed to go with me to the ground, and commended me, rather than otherwise, for refusing the offer which had been made to me. "I knew it would be so," he said, kindly; "I told my father you wouldn't. A man with the blood of the FOGARTIES, PHIL, my boy, doesn't wheel about like those fellows of yesterday." So, when CAMBACÈRES came out, which he did presently, with a more furious air than before, I handed him at once over to EUGÈNE, who begged him to name a friend, and an early hour for the meeting to take place.

"Can you make it before eleven, PHIL?" said BEAUHARNAIS. "The EMPEROR reviews the troops in the Bois de Boulogne at that hour, and we might fight there handy before the review."

"Done!" said I. "I want of all things to see the newly-arrived Saxon cavalry manœuvre:" on which CAMBACÈRES gave me a look, as much as to say, "See Sights! Watch Cavalry manœuvres! Make your soul, and take measure for a coffin, my boy!" walked away, naming our mutual acquaintance, MARSHAL NEY, to EUGÈNE, as his second in the business.

I had purchased from MURAT a very fine Irish horse, *Bugaboo*, out of *Smithereens*, by *Fadladeen*, which ran into the French ranks at Salamanca, with poor JACK CLONAKILTY, of the 13th, dead, on the top of him. *Bugaboo* was too much and too ugly an animal for the KING OF NAPLES, who, though a showy horseman, was a bad rider across country; and I got the horse for a song. A wickeder and uglier brute never wore pig-skin; and I never put my leg over such a timber-jumper in my life. I rode the horse down to the Bois de Boulogne on the morning that the affair with CAMBACÈRES was to come off, and LANTY held him as I went in, "sure to win," as they say in the ring.

CAMBACÈRES was known to be the best shot in the French army; but I, who am a pretty good hand at a snipe, thought a man was bigger, and that I could wing him if I had a mind. As soon as NEY gave the word, we both fired: I felt a whizz past my left ear, and putting up my hand there, found a large piece of my whiskers gone; whereas at the same moment, and shrieking a horrible malediction, my adversary reeled and fell.

"*Mon Dieu, il est mort!*" cried NEY.

"*Pas de tout,*" said BEAUHARNAIS. "*Écoute; il jure toujours.*"

And such, indeed, was the fact: the supposed dead man lay on the ground cursing most frightfully. We went up to him: he was blind with the loss of blood, and my ball had carried off the bridge of his nose. He recovered; but he was always called the Prince of Ponterotto in the French army, afterwards. The surgeon in attendance having taken charge of this unfortunate warrior, we rode off to the review, where NEY and EUGÈNE were on duty at the head of their respective divisions, and where, by the way, CAMBACÈRES, as the French say, "*se faisait désirer.*"

It was arranged that CAMBACÈRES' division of

six battalions and nine-and-twenty squadrons should execute a *ricochet* movement, supported by artillery in the intervals, and converging by different *épaulements* on the light infantry, that formed, as usual, the centre of the line. It was by this famons monœuvre that at Arcola, at Montenotte, at Friedland, and subsequently at Mazagran, SUWAROFF, PRINCE CHARLES, and GENERAL CASTANOS were defeated with such victorious slaughter: but it is a movement which, I need not tell every military man, requires the greatest delicacy of execution, and which, if it fails, plunges an army into confusion.

"Where is the DUKE OF ILLYRIA?" NAPOLEON asked. "At the head of his division, no doubt," said MURAT: at which EUGÈNE, giving me an arch look, put his hand to his nose, and caused me almost to fall off my horse with laughter. NAPOLEON looked sternly at me; but at this moment the troops getting in motion, the celebrated manœuvre began, and His Majesty's attention was taken off from my impudence.

MILHAUD'S Dragoons, their bands playing *Vive Henri Quatre*, their cuirasses gleaming in the sunshine, moved upon their own centre from the left flank in the most brilliant order, while the Carbineers of FOY, and the Grenadiers of the Guard under DROUET D'ERLON, executed a carambolade on the right, with the precision which became those veteran troops; but the Chasseurs of the young guard, marching by twos instead of threes, bore consequently upon the Bavarian Uhlans (an ill-disciplined and ill-affected body), and then, falling back in disorder, became entangled with the artillery and the left centre of the line, and in one instant thirty thousand men were in inextricable confusion.

"Clubbed, by Jabers!" roared out LANTY CLANCY. "I wish we could show 'em the Fighting Onety-oneth, Captain, darling."

"Silence, fellow!" I exclaimed. I never saw the face of man express passion so vividly as now did the livid countenance of NAPOLEON. He tore off GENERAL MILHAUD's epaulettes, which he flung into FOY's face. He glared about him wildly like a demon, and shouted hoarsely for the DUKE OF ILLYRIA. "He is wounded, Sire," said GENERAL FOY, wiping a tear from his eye, which was blackened by the force of the blow; "he was wounded an hour hence in a duel, Sire, by a young English prisoner, MONSIEUR DE FOGARTY."

"Wounded! a Marshal of France wounded! Where is the Englishman? Bring him out, and let a file of grenadiers"—

"Sire!" interposed EUGÈNE.

"Let him be shot!" shrieked the EMPEROR, shaking his spy-glass at me with the fury of a fiend.

This was too much. "Here goes!" said I, and rode slap at him.

There was a shriek of terror from the whole of the French army, and I should think at least forty thousand guns were levelled at me in an instant. But as the muskets were not loaded, and the cannon had only wadding in them, these facts, I presume, saved the life of PHIL FOGARTY from this discharge.

Knowing my horse, I put him at the EMPEROR's head, and *Bugaboo* went at it like a shot. He was riding his famous white Arab, and turned quite pale as I came up and went over the horse and the EMPEROR, scarcely brushing the cockade which he wore.

"Bravo!" said MURAT, bursting into enthusiasm at the leap.

"Cut him down!" said SIEYÈS, once an Abbé, but now a gigantic Cuirassier; and he made a pass at me with his sword. But he little knew an Irishman on an Irish horse. *Bugaboo* cleared SIEYÈS, and fetched the monster a slap with his near hind hoof which sent him reeling from his saddle,—and away I went, with an army of a hundred-and-seventy-three thousand eight hundred men at my heels. * * * * *

BARBAZURE.

BY G. P. R. JEAMES, ESQ., ETC.

I.

It was upon one of those balmy evenings of November which are only known in the valleys of Languedoc and among the mountains of Alsace, that two cavaliers might have been perceived by the naked eye threading one of the rocky and romantic gorges that skirt the mountain-land between the Marne and the Garonne. The rosy tints of the declining luminary were gilding the peaks and crags which lined the path, through which the horsemen wound slowly; and as those eternal battlements with which Nature had hemmed in the ravine which our travellers trod, blushed with the last tints of the fading sunlight, the valley below was grey and darkling, and the hard and devious course was sombre in twilight. A few goats, hardly visible among the peaks, were cropping the scanty herbage here and there. The pipes of shepherds, calling in their flocks as they trooped homewards to their mountain villages, sent up plaintive echoes which moaned through those rocky and lonely steeps; the stars began to glimmer in the purple heavens, spread serenely over head; and the faint crescent of the moon, which had peered for some time scarce visible in the azure, gleamed out more brilliantly at every moment, until it blazed as if in triumph at the sun's retreat. 'Tis a fair land that of France, a gentle, a green, and a beautiful; the home of arts and arms, of chivalry and romance, and (however sadly stained by the excesses of modern times) 'twas the unbought grace of nations once, and the seat of ancient renown and disciplined valour.

And of all that fair land of France, whose beauty is so bright, and bravery so famous, there is no spot greener or fairer than that one over which our travellers wended, and which stretches between the good towns of Vendemiaire and Nivose. 'Tis common now to a hundred thousand voyagers: the English tourist, with his chariot and his HARVEY'S Sauce, and his imperials; the bustling *commis-voyageur* on the roof of the rumbling diligence; the rapid *malle-poste* thundering over the *chaussée* at twelve miles an hour—pass the ground hourly and daily now: 'twas lonely and unfrequented at the end of that seventeenth century with which our story commences.

Along the darkening mountain paths the two gentlemen (for such their outward bearing proclaimed them) caracolled together. The one, seemingly the younger of the twain, wore a flaunting feather in his barret-cap, and managed a prancing Andalusian palfrey that bounded and curvetted gaily. A surcoat of peach-coloured samite and a purfled doublet of vair bespoke him noble, as did his brilliant eye, his exquisitely chiselled nose, and his curling chestnut ringlets.

Youth was on his brow; his eyes were dark and dewy, like spring-violets; and spring-roses bloomed upon his cheek—roses, alas! that bloom and die with life's spring! Now bounding over a rock, now playfully whisking off with his riding-rod a flowret in his path, PHILIBERT DE COQUELICOT rode by his darker companion.

His comrade was mounted upon a *destrière* of the true Norman breed, that had first champed grass on the green pastures of Acquitaine. Thence through Berry, Picardy, and the Limousin, halting at many a city and commune, holding joust and tourney in many a castle and manor of Navarre, Poitou, and St. Germain l'Auxerrois, the warrior and his charger reached the lonely spot where now we find them.

The warrior who bestrode the noble beast was in sooth worthy of the steed which bore him. Both were caparisoned in the fullest trappings of feudal war. The arblast, the mangonel, the demiculverin, and the cuissart of the period, glittered upon the neck and chest of the war-steed; while the rider, with chamfron and catapult, with ban and arrière-ban, morion and tumbril, battle-axe and rifflard, and the other appurtenances of ancient chivalry, rode stately on his steel-clad charger, himself a tower of steel. This mighty horseman was carried by his steed as lightly as the young springald by his Andalusian hackney.

"'Twas well done of thee, PHILIBERT;" said he of the proof-armour, "to ride forth so far to welcome thy cousin and companion in arms."

"Companion in battledoor and shuttlecock, ROMANÉ DE CLOS-VOUGEOT!" replied the younger Cavalier. "When I was yet a page, thou wert a belted knight; and thou wert away to the Crusades ere ever my beard grew."

"I stood by RICHARD of England at the gates of Ascalon, and drew the spear from sainted KING LOUIS in the tents of Damietta," the individual addressed as ROMANÉ replied. "Well-a-day! since thy beard grew, boy, (and marry 'tis yet a thin one,) I have broken a lance with SOLYMAN at Rhodes, and smoked a chibouque with SALADIN at Acre. But enough of this. Tell me of home—of our native valley—of my hearth, and my lady mother, and my good chaplain—tell me of *her*, PHILIBERT," said the knight, executing a demivolte, in order to hide his emotion.

PHILIBERT seemed uneasy, and to strive as though he would parry the question. "The castle stands on the rock," he said, "and the swallows still build in the battlements. The good chaplain still chants his vespers at morn, and snuffles his matins at even-song. The lady-mother still distributeth tracts, and knitteth Berlin linsey-woolsey. The tenants pay no better, and the lawyers dun as sorely, kinsman mine," he added with an arch look.

"But FATIMA, FATIMA, how fares she?" ROMANÉ continued—"Since Lammas was a twelvemonth, I hear nought of her; my letters are unanswered. The postman hath traversed our camp every day, and never brought me a billet. How is FATIMA, PHILIBERT DE COQUELICOT?"

"She is—well," PHILIBERT replied; "her sister ANNE is the fairest of the twain, though."

"Her sister ANNE was a baby when I embarked for Egypt. A plague on sister ANNE! Speak of FATIMA, PHILIBERT—my blue-eyed FATIMA!"

"I say she is—well," answered his comrade, gloomily.

"Is she dead? Is she ill? Hath she the measles? Nay, hath she had small-pox, and lost her beauty? Speak! speak, boy!" cried the knight, wrought to agony.

"Her cheek is as red as her mother's, though the old Countess paints hers every day. Her foot is as light as a sparrow's, and her voice as sweet as a minstrel's dulcimer; but give me nathless the LADY ANNE," cried PHILIBERT, "give me the peerless LADY

ANNE! As soon as ever I have won spurs, I will ride all Christendom through, and proclaim her the Queen of Beauty. Ho, LADY ANNE! LADY ANNE!" and so saying—but evidently wishing to disguise some emotion, or conceal some tale his friend could ill brook to hear—the reckless *damoiseau* galloped wildly forward.

But swift as was his courser's pace, that of his companion's enormous charger was swifter. "Boy," said the elder, "thou hast ill tidings. I know it by thy glance. Speak: shall he who hath bearded grim Death in a thousand fields shame to face truth from a friend? Speak, in the name of Heaven and good SAINT BOTIBOL. ROMANÉ DE CLOS-VOUGEOT will bear your tidiings like a man!"

"FATIMA is well," answered PHILIBERT once again; "she hath had no measles: she lives and is still fair."

"Fair, aye, peerless fair; but what more, PHILIBERT? Not false? By SAINT BOTIBOL, say not false," groaned the elder warrior.

"A month syne," PHILIBERT replied, "she married the BARON DE BARBAZURE."

With that scream which is so terrible in a strong man in agony, the brave knight ROMANÉ DE CLOS-VOUGEOT sank back at the words, and fell from his charger to the ground, a lifeless mass of steel.

II.

Like many another fabric of feudal war and splendour, the once vast and magnificent Castle of Barbazure is now a moss-grown ruin. The traveller of the present day, who wanders by the banks of the silvery Loire, and climbs the steep on which the magnificent edifice stood, can scarcely trace, among the shattered masses of ivy-covered masonry which lie among the lonely crags, even the skeleton of the proud and majestic palace-stronghold of the Barons of Barbazure.

In the days of our tale its turrets and pinnacles rose as stately, and seemed (to the pride of sinful man!) as strong as the eternal rocks on which they stood. The three mullets on a gules wavy reversed, surmounted by the sinople couchant Or; the well-known cognizance of the house, blazed in gorgeous heraldry on a hundred banners, surmounting as many towers. The long lines of battlemented walls spread down the mountain to the Loire, and were defended by thousands of steel-clad serving-men. Four hundred knights and six times as many archer's fought round the banner of Barbazure at Bouvines, Malplaquet, and Azincour. For his services at Fontenoy against the English, the heroic Charles Martel appointed the fourteenth Baron Hereditary Grand Bootjack of the kingdom of France; and for wealth, for splendour, and for skill and fame in war, RAOUL the twenty-eighth Baron, was in no wise inferior to his noble ancestors.

That the BARON RAOUL levied toll upon the river, and mail upon the shore; that he now and then ransomed a burgher, plundered a neighbour, or drew the fangs of a Jew; that he burned an enemy's castle with the wife and children within;—these were points for which the country knew and respected the stout Baron. When he returned from victory, he was sure to endow the Church with a part of his spoil, so that when he went forth to battle he was always accompanied by her blessing. Thus lived the BARON RAOUL, the pride of the country in which he dwelt, an ornament to the Court, the Church, and his neighbours.

But in the midst of all his power and splendour there was a domestic grief which deeply afflicted the princely BARBAZURE. His lovely ladies died one after the other. No sooner was he married than he was a widower; in the course of eighteen years no less than nine bereavements had befallen the chieftain. So true it is, that if fortune is a parasite, grief is a republican, and visits the hall of the great and wealthy as it does the humbler tenements of the poor.

* * * * * * * * *

"Leave off deploring thy faithless, gad-about lover," said the Lady of Chacabacque to her daughter, the lovely FATIMA, "and think how the noble BARBAZURE loves thee! Of all the damsels at the ball last night, he had eyes for thee and thy cousin only."

"I am sure my cousin hath no good looks to be proud of!" the admirable FATIMA exclaimed, bridling up. "Not that *I* care for my LORD OF BARBAZURE's looks. *My* heart, dearest mother, is with him who is far away!"

"He danced with thee four galliards, nine quadrilles, and twenty-three corantoes, I think, child," the mother said, eluding her daughter's remark.

"Twenty-five," said lovely FATIMA, casting her beautiful eyes to the ground. "Heigh-ho! but ROMANÉ danced them very well!"

"He had not the court air," the mother suggested.

"I don't wish to deny the beauty of the LORD OF BARBAZURE's dancing, Mamma," FATIMA replied. "For a short, lusty man, 'tis wondrous how active he is; and in dignity the King's Grace himself could not surpass him."

"You were the noblest couple in the room, love," the lady cried.

"That pea-green doublet, slashed with orange-tawney, those ostrich plumes, blue, red, and yellow, those parti-coloured hose and pink shoon became the noble Baron wondrous well," FATIMA acknowledged. "It must be confessed that, though middle-aged, he hath all the agility of youth. But, alas! Madam! The noble Baron hath had nine wives already."

"And your cousin would give her eyes to become the tenth," the mother replied.

"My cousin give her eyes!" FATIMA exclaimed. "It's not much, I'm sure, for she squints abominably;" and thus the ladies prattled, as they rode home at night after the great ball at the house of the BARON OF BARBAZURE.

The gentle reader, who has overheard their talk, will understand the doubts which pervaded the mind of the lovely FATIMA, and the well-nurtured English maiden will participate in the divided feelings which rent her bosom. 'Tis true, that on his departure for the holy wars, ROMANÉ and FATIMA were plighted to each other; but the folly of long engagements is proverbial; and though for many months the faithful and affectionate girl had looked in vain for news from him, her admirable parents had long spoken with repugnance of a match which must bring inevitable poverty to both parties. They had suffered, 'tis true, the engagement to subside, hostile as they ever were to it; but when at the death of the ninth lady of BARBAZURE, the noble Baron remarked FATIMA at the funeral, and rode home with her after the ceremony, her prudent parents saw how much wiser, better, happier, for their child it would be to have for life a partner like the Baron, than to wait the doubtful return of the penniless wanderer to whom she was plighted.

Ah! how beautiful and pure a being! how regardless of self! how true to duty! how obedient to parental command, is that earthly angel, a well-bred woman of genteel family! Instead of indulging in splenetic refusals or vain regrets for her absent lover, the exemplary FATIMA at once signified to her excellent parents her willingness to obey their orders; though she had sorrows (and she declared them to be tremendous), the admirable being disguised them so well, that none knew they oppressed her. She said she would try to forget former ties, and (so strong in her mind was *duty* above every other feeling; so strong may it be in every British maiden!) the lovely girl kept her promise. "My former engagements," she said, packing up ROMANÉ's letters and presents, (which, as the good knight was mortal poor, were in sooth of no great price)—"my former engagements I look upon as childish follies;—my affections are fixed where my dear parents graft them—on the noble, the princely, the polite BARBAZURE. 'Tis true he is not comely in feature, but the chaste and well-bred female knows how to despise the fleeting charms of form. 'Tis true he is old; but can woman be better employed than in tending her aged and sickly companion? That he has been married is likewise certain—but ah, my mother! who knows not that he must be a good and tender husband, who, nine times wedded, owns that he cannot be happy without another partner?"

It was with these admirable sentiments the lovely Fatima proposed obedience to her parents' will, and consented to receive the magnificent marriage gift presented to her by her gallant bridegroom.

III.

The old Countess of Chacabacque had made a score of vain attempts to see her hapless daughter. Ever, when she came, the porters grinned at her savagely through the grating of the portcullis of the vast embattled gate of the Castle of Barbazure, and rudely bade her begone. "The Lady of Barbazure sees nobody but her confessor, and keeps her chamber," was the invariable reply of the dogged functionaries to the entreaties of the agonised mother. And at length, so furious was he at her perpetual calls at his gate, that the angry Lord of Barbazure himself, who chanced to be at the postern, armed a cross-bow, and let fly an arblast at the crupper of the lady's palfrey, whereon she fled finally, screaming and in terror. "I will aim at the rider next time!" howled the ferocious Baron, "and not at the horse!" And those who knew his savage nature and his unrivalled skill as a bowman, knew that he would neither break his knightly promise nor miss his aim.

Since the fatal day when the Grand Duke of Burgundy gave his famous passage of arms at Nantes, and all the nobles of France were present at the joustings, it was remarked that the BARBAZURE's heart was changed towards his gentle and virtuous lady.

For the three first days of that famous festival, the redoubted BARON OF BARBAZURE had kept the field against all the knights who entered. His lance bore everything down before it. The most famous champions of Europe, assembled at these joustings, had dropped, one by one, before this tremendous warrior. The prize of the tourney was destined to be his, and he was to be proclaimed bravest of the brave, as his lady was the fairest of the fair.

On the third day, however, as the sun was declining over the Vosges, and the shadows were lengthening over the plain where the warrior had obtained such triumphs;—after having overcome two hundred and thirteen knights of different nations, including the fiery DUNOIS, the intrepid WALTER MANNY, the spotless BAYARD, and the undaunted DUGUESCLIN, as the conqueror sate still erect on his charger, and the multitudes doubted whether ever another champion could be found to face him, three blasts of a trumpet were heard, faint at first, but at every moment ringing more clearly, until a knight in pink armour rode into the lists with his visor down, and riding a tremendous dun charger, which he managed to the admiration of all present.

The heralds asked him his name and quality.

"Call me," said he, in a hollow voice, "the Jilted Knight." What was it made the LADY OF BARBAZURE tremble at his accents?

The knight refused to tell his name and qualities; but the companion who rode with him, the young and noble PHILIBERT DE COQUELICOT, who was known and respected universally through the neighbourhood, gave a warranty for the birth and noble degree of the Jilted Knight—and RAOUL DE BARBAZURE, yelling hoarsely for a two hundred and fourteenth lance, shook the huge weapon in the air as though it were a reed, and prepared to encounter the intruder.

According to the wont of chivalry, and to keep the point of the spear from harm, the top of the unknown knight's lance was shielded with a bung, which the warrior removed; and galloping up to BARBAZURE's pavilion, over which his shield hung, touched that noble cognizance with the sharpened steel. A thrill of excitement ran through the assembly at this daring challenge to a combat *à l'outrance.* "Hast thou confessed, Sir Knight?" roared the BARBAZURE; "take thy ground, and look to thyself; for by Heaven thy last hour is come!" Poor youth, poor youth!

sighed the spectators; he has called down his own fate. The next minute the signal was given, and as the simoom across the desert, the cataract down the rock, the shell from the howitzer, each warrior rushed from his goal. * * * * * *

"Thou wilt not slay so good a champion!" said the Grand Duke, as at the end of that terrific combat the knight in rose armour stood over his prostrate foe, whose helmet had rolled off when he was at length unhorsed, and whose blood-shot eyes glared unutterable hate and ferocity on his conqueror.

"Take thy life," said he who had styled himself the Jilted Knight; "thou hast taken all that was dear to me;" and the sun setting, and no other warrior appearing to do battle against him, he was proclaimed the conqueror, and rode up to the duchess' balcony to receive the gold chain which was the reward of the victor. He raised his visor as the smiling princess guerdoned him—raised it, and gave *one* sad look towards the Lady Fatima at her side!"

"Romané de Clos Vougeot!" shrieked she, and fainted. The Baron of Barbazure heard the name as he writhed on the ground with his wound, and by his slighted honour, by his broken ribs, by his roused fury, he swore revenge; and the Lady Fatima, who had come to the tourney as a Queen, returned to her castle as a prisoner.

(As it is impossible to give in the limits of our

periodical the whole of this remarkable novel, let it suffice to say briefly here, that in about a volume and a half, in which the descriptions of scenery, the account of the agonies of the Baroness kept on bread and water in her dungeon, and the general tone of morality, are all excellently worked out; the BARON DE BARBAZURE resolves upon putting his wife to death by the hands of the public executioner.)

* * * * * * * *

Two minutes before the clock struck noon, the savage Baron was on the platform to inspect the preparation for the frightful ceremony of mid-day.

The block was laid forth—the hideous minister of vengeance, masked, and in black, with the flaming glaive in his hand, was ready. The Baron tried the edge of the blade with his finger, and asked the dreadful swordsman if his hand was sure? A nod was the reply of the man of blood. The weeping garrison and domestics shuddered and shrank from him. There was not one there but loved and pitied the gentle lady.

Pale, pale as a stone, she was brought from her dungeon. To all her lord's savage interrogatories, her reply had been, "I am innocent." To his threats of death, her answer was, "You are my lord; my life is in your hands, to take or to give." How few are the wives, in our day, who show such angelic meekness! It touched all hearts around her, save that of the implacable BARBAZURE! Even the LADY BLANCHE, (FATIMA's cousin,) whom he had promised to marry upon his faithless wife's demise, besought for her kinswoman's life, and a divorce; but BARBAZURE had vowed her death.

"Is there no pity, Sir?" asked the chaplain who had attended her. "No pity," echoed the weeping serving-maid. "Did I not aye say I would die for my lord?" said the gentle lady, and placed herself at the block.

SIR RAOUL DE BARBAZURE seized up the long ringlets of her raven hair. "Now!" shouted he to the executioner, with a stamp of his foot, "Now strike!"

The man (who knew his trade) advanced at once, and poised himself to deliver his blow: and making his flashing sword sing in the air, with one irresistible, rapid stroke, it sheared clean off the head of the furious, the blood-thirsty, the implacable BARON DE BARBAZURE!

Thus he fell a victim to his own jealousy; and the agitation of the LADY FATIMA may be imagined, when the executioner, flinging off his mask, knelt gracefully at her feet, and revealed to her the well-known features of ROMANÉ DE CLOS VOUGEOT.

LORDS AND LIVERIES.

BY THE AUTHORESS OF "DUKES AND DEJEUNERS," "HEARTS AND DIAMONDS," "MARCHIONESSES AND MILLINERS," ETC. ETC.

I.

Corbleu! What a lovely creature that was in the Fitzbattleaxe box to-night," said one of a group of young dandies, who were leaning over the velvet-cushioned balconies of the Coventry Club, smoking their full-flavoured Cubas (from Hudson's) after the opera.

Everybody stared at such an exclamation of enthusiasm from the lips of the young Earl of Bagnigge, who was never heard to admire anything except a *coulis de dindonneau à la St. Ménéhould*, or a *suprême de cochon en torticolis à la Piffarde;* such as Champollion, the chief of the Travellers, only knows how to dress; or the *bouquet* of a flask of Médoc, of Carbonell's best quality; or a *goutte* of Marasquin, from the cellars of Briggs and Hobson.

Alured de Pentonville, eighteenth Earl of Bagnigge, Viscount Paon of Islington, Baron Pancras, Kingscross, and a Baronet, was, like too many of our young men of *ton*, utterly *blasé*, although only in his twenty-fourth year. Blest, luckily, with a mother of excellent principles, (who had imbued his young mind with that Morality which is so superior to all the vain pomps of the world !), it had not been always the young Earl's lot to wear the coronet for which he now in sooth cared so little. His father, a Captain of Britain's navy, struck down by the side of the gallant COLLINGWOOD in the Bay of Fundy, left little but his sword and spotless name to his young, lovely, and inconsolable widow, who passed the first years of her mourning in educating her child in an elegant though small cottage in one of the romantic marine villages of beautiful Devonshire. Her child ! What a gush of consolation filled the widow's heart as she pressed him to it ! how faithfully did she instil into his young bosom those principles which had been the pole-star of the existence of his gallant father.

In this secluded retreat, rank and wealth almost boundless found the widow and her boy. The seventeenth Earl—gallant and ardent, and in the prime of youth—went forth one day from the Eternal City to a steeple-chase in the Campagna. A mutilated corpse was brought back to his hotel in the Piazza de Spagna. Death, alas ! is no respecter of the Nobility. That shattered form was all that remained of the fiery, the haughty, the wild, but the generous ALTAMONT DE PENTONVILLE ! Such, such is fate !

The admirable EMILY DE PENTONVILLE trembled

with all a mother's solicitude at the distinctions and honours which thus suddenly descended on her boy. She engaged an excellent clergyman of the Church of England to superintend his studies; to accompany him on foreign travel when the proper season arrived; to ward from him those dangers which dissipation always throws in the way of the noble, the idle, and the wealthy. But the REVEREND CYRIL DELAVAL died of the measles at Naples, and henceforth the young EARL OF BAGNIGGE was without a guardian.

What was the consequence? That, at three-and-twenty, he was a cynic and an epicure. He had drained the cup of pleasure until it had palled in his unnerved hand. He had looked at the Pyramids without awe, at the Alps without reverence. He was unmoved by the sandy solitudes of the desert as by the placid depths of Mediterranea's sea of blue. Bitter, bitter tears did EMILY DE PENTONVILLE weep, when, on ALURED's return from the Continent, she beheld the awful change that dissipation had wrought in her beautiful, her blue-eyed, her perverted, her still beloved boy!

"Corpo di bacco," he said, pitching the end of his cigar on to the red nose of the COUNTESS OF DELAWADDYMORE's coachman, who, having deposited her fat ladyship at No. 236, Piccadilly, was driving the carriage to the stables, before commencing his evening at the Fortune of War public-house; "what a lovely creature that was! What eyes! what hair! Who knows her? Do you, *mon cher Prince?*

"*E bellissima, certamente,*" said the DUCA DI MONTEPULCIANO, and stroked down his jetty moustache.

"*Ein gar schönes Mädchen,*" said the HEREDITARY GRAND DUKE OF EULENSCHRECKENSTEIN, and turned up his carroty one.

"*Elle n'est pas mal, ma foi!*" said the PRINCE DE BORODINO, with a scowl on his darkling brows. "*Mon Dieu, que ces cigarres sont mauvais!*" he added, as he too cast away his Cuba.

"Try one of my Pickwicks," said FRANKLIN FOX, with a sneer, offering his gold *étui* to the young Frenchman; "they are some of PONTET's best, Prince. What, do you bear malice? Come, let us be friends," said the gay and careless young patrician; but a scowl on the part of the Frenchman was the only reply.

—"Want to know who she is? BORODINO knows who she is, BAGNIGGE," the wag went on.

Everybody crowded round MONSIEUR DE BORODINO thus apostrophised. The MARQUIS OF ALICOMPAYNE, young DE BOOTS of the Life Guards, TOM PROTOCOL of the Foreign Office; the gay young peers FARINTOSH, POLDOODY, and the rest; and BAGNIGGE, for a wonder, not less eager than any one present.

"No, he will tell you nothing about her. Don't you see he has gone off in a fury?" FRANKLIN FOX continued. "He has his reasons, *ce cher Prince:* he will tell you nothing; but I will. You know that I am *au mieux* with the dear old Duchess."

"They say FRANK and she are engaged after the Duke's death," cried POLDOODY.

"I always thought FWANK was the Duke's illicit gweat-gwandson," drawled out DE BOOTS.

"I heard that he doctored her Blenheim, and used to bring her wigs from Paris," cried that malicious TOM PROTOCOL, whose *mots* are known in every diplomatic *salon* from Petersburgh to Palermo.

"Burn her wigs, and hang her poodle!" said BAGNIGGE. "Tell us about this girl, FRANKLIN FOX?"

"In the first place, she has five hundred thousand acres, in a ring fence, in Norfolk; a County in Scotland, a Castle in Wales, a Villa at Richmond, a corner house in Belgrave-square, and eighty thousand a year in the Three per Cents."

"*Après?*" said BAGNIGGE, still yawning.

"Secondly, BORODINO *lui fait la cour.* They are cousins, her mother was an Armagnac of the emigration; the old Marshal, his father, married another sister. I believe he was footman in the family, before NAPOLEON princified him."

"No, no, he was second coachman"—TOM PRO-

TOCOL good-naturedly interposed—"a cavalry officer, FRANK, not an infantry man."

"Faith, you should have seen his fury (the young one's, I mean) when he found me in the Duchess's room this evening, *tête-à-tête* with the heiress, who deigned to accept a *bouquet* from this hand."

"It cost me three guineas," poor FRANK said, with a shrug and a sigh, "and that Covent Garden scoundrel gives no credit: but she took the flowers;—eh, BAGNIGGE?"

"And flung them to ALBONI," the Peer replied, with a haughty sneer. And poor little FRANKLIN FOX was compelled to own that she had.

The *maître-d'hôtel* here announced that supper was served. It was remarked that even the *coulis de dindonneau* made no impression on BAGNIGGE that night.

II.

THE sensation produced by the *débût* of AMETHYST PIMLICO at the Court of the Sovereign, and in the *salons* of the *beau-monde*, was such as has seldom been created by the appearance of any other beauty. The men were raving with love, and the women with jealousy. Her eyes, her beauty, her wit, her grace, her *ton*, caused a perfect *fureur* of admiration or envy.

Introduced by the DUCHESS OF FITZBATTLEAXE, along with her Grace's daughters, the Ladies GWENDOLINE and GWINEVER PORTCULLIS, the heiress's regal beauty quite flung her cousins' simple charms into the shade, and blazed with a splendour which caused all "minor lights" to twinkle faintly. Before a day the *beau-monde*, before a week even the vulgarians of the rest of the town, rang with the fame of her charms; and while the dandies and the beauties were raving about her, or tearing her to pieces in May Fair, even MRS. DOBBS (who had been to the pit of the "Hoperer" in a green turban and a crumpled yellow satin), talked about the great *hairess* to her D. in Bloomsbury Square.

Crowds went to SQUAB AND LYNCH'S, in Long Acre, to examine the carriages building for her, so faultless, so splendid, so quiet, so odiously unostentatious and provokingly simple! Besides the ancestral services of *argenterie* and *vaisselle plate*, contained in a hundred and seventy six plate chests at MESSRS. CHILDS'; RUMBLE and BRIGGS prepared a gold service, and GARRAWAY, of the Haymarket, a service of the BENVENUTO CELLINI pattern, which were the admiration of all London. Before a month it is a fact that the wretched haberdashers in the city exhibited blue stocks, called "Heiress-killers, very chaste, two-and-six;" long before that, the *monde* had rushed to MADAME CRINOLINE'S, or sent couriers to MADAME MARABOU, at Paris, so as to have copies of her dresses; but, as the Mantuan bard observes, "*Non cuivis contigit*,"—every foot cannot accommodate itself to the *chaussure* of CINDERELLA.

With all this splendour, this worship, this beauty; with these cheers following her, and these crowds at her feet, was AMETHYST happy? Ah, no! It is not under the necklace the most brilliant that BRIGGS and RUMBLE can supply; it is not in LYNCH's best cushioned chariot that the heart is most at ease. "*Que je me ruinerai*," says FRONSAC in a letter to BOSSUET, "*si je savais où acheter le bonheur!*"

With all her riches, with all her splendour, AMETHYST was wretched — wretched, because lonely; wretched, because her loving heart had nothing to cling to. Her splendid mansion was a convent; no male person ever entered it, except FRANKLIN FOX, (who counted for nothing,) and the Duchess's family, her kinsman old LORD HUMPINGTON, his friend old SIR JOHN FOGEY, and her cousin, the odious, odious BORODINO.

The PRINCE DE BORODINO declared openly that AMETHYST was engaged to him. *Criblé de dettes*, it is no wonder that he should choose such an opportunity to *refaire sa fortune*. He gave out that he would kill any man who should cast an eye on the heiress, and the monster kept his word. MAJOR

GRIGG, of the Life Guards, had already fallen by his hand at Ostend. The O'TOOLE, who had met her on the Rhine, had received a ball in his shoulder at Coblentz, and did not care to resume so dangerous a courtship. BORODINO could snuff a *bougie* at a hundred-and-fifty yards. He could beat BERTRAND or ALEXANDER DUMAS himself with the small sword; he was the dragon that watched this *pomme d'or*, and very few persons were now inclined to face a champion *si redoutable.*

Over a *Salmi d' escargot* at the Coventry, the dandies whom we introduced in our last volume were assembled, there talking of the heiress: and her story was told by FRANKLIN FOX to LORD BAGNIGGE, who, for a wonder, was interested in the tale. BORODINO'S pretensions were discussed, and the way in which the fair AMETHYST was confined. Fitzbattleaxe House, in Belgrave Square, is—as every body knows—the next mansion to that occupied by AMETHYST. A communication was made between the two houses. She never went out except accompanied by the Duchess's guard, which it was impossible to overcome.

"Impossible! Nothing's impossible," said LORD BAGNIGGE.

"I bet you what you like you don't get in," said the young MARQUIS OF MARTINGALE.

"I bet you a thousand ponies I stop a week in the heiress's house before the season's over," LORD BAG-

NIGGE replied with a yawn; and the bet was registered with shouts of applause.

But it seemed as if the Fates had determined against Lord BAGNIGGE, for the very next day, riding in the Park, his horse fell with him; he was carried home to his house with a fractured limb and a dislocated shoulder; and the doctor's bulletins pronounced him to be in the most dangerous state.

MARTINGALE was a married man, and there was no danger of *his* riding by the FITZBATTLEAXE carriage. A fortnight after the above events, his Lordship was prancing by her Grace's great family coach, and chattering with LADY GWINEVER about the strange wager.

"Do you know what a poney is, LADY GWINEVER?" he asked. Her Ladyship said yes; she had a cream-coloured one at Castle Barbican; and stared when LORD MARTINGALE announced that he should soon have a thousand ponies, worth five-and-twenty pounds each, which were all now kept at COUTTS'S. Then he explained the circumstances of the bet with BAGNIGGE. Parliament was to adjourn in ten days; the season would be over; BAGNIGGE was lying ill *chez lui;* and the five-and-twenty thousand were irrecoverably his. And he vowed he would buy LORD BINNACLE'S yacht—crew, captain, guns and all.

On returning home that night from LADY POLKIMORE'S, MARTINGALE found among the many *billets* upon the gold *plateau* in his *antichambre*, the following brief one, which made him start:—

"DEAR MARTINGALE,—Don't be too sure of BINNACLE'S yacht. There are still ten days before the season is over; and my ponies may lie at COUTTS'S for some time to come. "Yours,

"BAGNIGGE."

"P. S.—I write with my left hand; for my right is still splintered up from that confounded fall."

III.

THE tall footman, number four, who had come in the place of JOHN, cashiered (for want of proper *mollets*, and because his hair did not take powder well), had given great satisfaction to the under-butler, who reported well of him to his chief, who had mentioned his name with praise to the house-steward. He was so good-looking and well-spoken a young man, that the ladies in the housekeeper's room deigned to notice him more than once; nor was his popularity diminished on account of a quarrel in which he engaged with MONSIEUR ANATOLE, the enormous Walloon *chasseur*, who was one day found embracing MISS FLOUNCY, who waited on AMETHYST'S own maid. The very instant

MISS FLOUNCY saw MR. JEAMES entering the Servant's Hall, where MONSIEUR ANATOLE was engaged in "aggravating" her, MISS FLOUNCY screamed—at the next moment the Belgian giant lay sprawling upon the carpet—and JEAMES, standing over him, assumed so terrible a look, that the *chasseur* declined any further combat. The victory was made known to the house-steward himself, who being a little partial to MISS FLOUNCY herself, complimented JEAMES on his valour, and poured out a glass of Madeira in his own room.

Who was JEAMES? He had come recommended by the BAGNIGGE people. He had lived, he said, in that family two years. "But where there was no ladies," he said, "a gentleman's hand was spiled for service;" and JEAMES's was a very delicate hand; MISS FLOUNCY admired it very much, and of course he did not defile it by menial service; he had in a young man who called him "Sir," and did all the coarse work; and JEAMES read the morning paper to the ladies; not spellingly and with hesitation, as many gentlemen do, but easily and elegantly, speaking off the longest words without a moment's difficulty. He could speak French, too, MISS FLOUNCY found, who was studying it under MADEMOISELLE, *grande fille-de-chambre de confiance;* for when she said to him "*Polly voo Fransy*, MUNSEER JEAMES?" he replied readily "*We, Mademaselle j'ay passay boco de tong à Parry. Commong voo potty voo ?*" How Miss Flouncy admired him as he stood before her, the day after he had saved Miss Amethyst when the horses had run away with her in the park!

Poor Flouncy, poor Flouncy! Jeames had been but a week in Amethyst's service, and already the gentle heart of the washing-girl was irrecoverably gone! Poor Flouncy! poor Flouncy! he thought not of thee.

It happened thus. Miss Amethyst being engaged to drive with her cousin the Prince in his phaeton, her own carriage was sent into the Park simply with her companion, who had charge of her little Fido, the dearest little spaniel in the world. Jeames and Frederick were behind the carriage with their long sticks and neat dark liveries; the horses were worth a thousand guineas each, the coachman a late Lieutenant-Colonel of cavalry: the whole ring could not boast a more elegant turn out.

The Prince drove his curricle and had charge of his *belle cousine.* It may have been the red fezzes in the carriage of the Turkish ambassador which frightened the Prince's greys, or Mrs. Champignon's new yellow liveries, which were flaunting in the Park, or hideous Lady Gorgon's preternatural ugliness, who passed in a low pony-carriage at the time, or the prince's own want of skill, finally; but certain it is that the horses took fright, dashed wildly along the mile, scattered equipages, *piétons*, dandies' cabs, and Snobs' *pheaytons*. Amethyst was screaming; and the Prince, deadly pale, had lost all presence of mind, as the curricle came rushing by the spot where Miss Amythist's carriage stood.

"I'm blest," Frederick exclaimed to his companion, "if it ain't the Prince a drivin our Missis! They'll be in the Serpingtine, or dashed to pieces, if they dont mind;" and the runaway steeds at this instant came upon them as a whirlwind.

But if those steeds ran at a whirlwind pace, Jeames was swifter. To jump from behind, to bound after the rocking, reeling curricle, to jump into it aided by the long stick which he carried and used as a leaping-pole, and to seize the reins out of the hands of the miserable Borodino, who shrieked piteously as the dauntless valet leapt on his toes and into his seat, was the work of an instant. In a few minutes the mad, swaying rush of the horses was reduced to a swift but steady gallop; presently into a canter, then a trot; until finally they pulled up smoking and trembling, but quite quiet, by the side of Amethyst's carriage, which came up at a rapid pace.

"Give me the reins, *malappris! tu m'écrases les cors, manant!*" yelled the frantic nobleman, writhing underneath the intrepid charioteer.

"*Tant pis pour toi, nigaud*," was the reply. The lovely Amethyst of course had fainted; but she recovered as she was placed in her carriage, and rewarded her preserver with a celestial smile.

The rage, the fury, the maledictions of BORODINO, as he saw the latter—a liveried menial—stoop gracefully forward and kiss AMETHYST's hand, may be imagined rather than described. But JEAMES heeded not his curses. Having placed his adored mistress in the carriage, he calmly resumed his station behind. Passion or danger seemed to have no impression upon that pale marble face.

BORODINO went home furious; nor was his rage diminished, when, on coming to dinner that day, a *recherché* banquet served in the *Frangipané* best style, and requesting a supply of a *purée à la bisque aux écrévisses*, the clumsy attendant who served him let fall the *assiette* of *vermeille ciselé* with its scalding contents, over the Prince's chin, his Mechlin *jabot* and the grand *cordon* of the Legion of Honour which he wore.

"*Infâme*," howled BORODINO, "*tu l'as fait exprès!*"

"*Oui, je l'ai fait exprès*," said the man, with the most perfect Parisian accent. It was JEAMES.

Such insolence of course could not be passed unnoticed even after the morning's service, and he was *chasséd* on the spot. He had been but a week in the house.

The next month the newspapers contained a paragraph which may possibly elucidate the above mystery, and to the following effect:—

Singular Wager.—One night, at the end of last season, the young and eccentric EARL OF B—GN—GGE laid a wager of twenty-five thousand pounds with a broken sporting patrician, the dashing MARQUIS OF M—RT—NG—LE, that he would pass a week under the roof of a celebrated and lovely young heiress, who lives not a hundred miles from B—LGR—VE SQU—RE. The bet having been made, the Earl pretended an illness, and having taken lessons from one of his lordship's own footmen (MR. JAMES PLUSH, whose name he also borrowed) in '*the mysteries* of the *profession*,' actually succeeded in making an entry into MISS P—ML—CO's mansion, where he stopped one week exactly; having time to win his bet, and to save the life of the lady, whom we hear he is about to lead to the altar. He disarmed the PRINCE OF BORODINO in a duel fought on Calais sands—and it is said, appeared at the C— club wearing his *plush costume* under a cloak, and displaying it as a proof that he had won his wager."

Such, indeed, were the circumstances. The young couple have not more than nine hundred thousand a year, but they live cheerfully, and manage to do good; and EMILY DE PENTONVILLE, who adores her daughter-in-law and her little grand-children, is blest in seeing her darling son *enfin un homme rangé.*

CODLINGSBY.

BY B. DE SHREWSBURY, ESQ.

I.

"THE whole world is bound by one chain. In every city in the globe there is one quarter that certain travellers know and recognize from its likeness to its brother district in all other places where are congregated the habitations of men. In Tehran, or Pekin, or Stamboul, or New York, or Timbuctoo, or London, there is a certain district where a certain man is not a stranger. Where the idols are fed with incense by the streams of Ching-wang-foo; where the minarets soar sparkling above the cypresses, their reflexions quivering in the lucid waters of the Golden Horn; where the yellow Tiber flows under broken bridges and over imperial glories; where the huts are squatted by the Niger, under the palm-trees; where the Northern Babel lies, with its warehouses, and its bridges, its graceful factory-chimneys, and its clumsy fanes—hidden in fog and smoke by the dirtiest river in the world—in all the cities of mankind there is One Home whither men of one family may resort. Over the entire world spreads a vast brotherhood, suffering, silent, scattered, sympathising, *waiting*—an immense Free-Masonry. Once this world-spread band was an Arabian clan—a little nation alone and outlying amongst the mighty monarchies of ancient time, the Megatheria of history. The sails of their rare ships might be seen in the Egyptian waters; the camels of their caravans might thread the sands of Baalbec, or wind through the date-groves of Damascus; their flag was raised, not ingloriously, in many wars, against mighty odds; but 'twas a small people, and on one dark night the Lion of Judah went down before VESPASIAN'S Eagles, and in flame, and death, and struggle, Jerusalem agonized and died. * * * Yes, the Jewish city is lost to Jewish men; but have they not taken the world in exchange?"

Mused thus GODFREY DE BOUILLON, MARQUIS OF CODLINGSBY, as he debouched from Wych Street into the Strand. He had been to take a box for ARMIDA at MADAME VESTRIS'S theatre. That little ARMIDA was *folle* of MADAME VESTRIS'S theatre; and her little Brougham, and her little self, and her enormous eyes, and her prodigious opera-glass, and her miraculous bouquet, which cost LORD CODLINGSBY twenty guineas every evening at NATHAN'S in Covent Garden, (the children of the gardeners of Sharon have still no rival for flowers,) might be seen three nights in the week at least, in the narrow, charming, comfortable little theatre. GODFREY had the box. He was strolling, listlessly, eastward; and the above thoughts passed through the young noble's mind as he came in sight of Holywell Street.

The occupants of the London Ghetto sat at their porches basking in the evening sunshine. Children were playing on the steps. Fathers were smoking at the lintel. Smiling faces looked out from the various and darkling draperies with which the warehouses were hung. Ringlets glossy, and curly, and jetty—eyes black as night—midsummer night—when it lightens; haughty noses bending like beaks of eagles—eager quivering nostrils—lips curved like the bow of Love—every man or maiden, every babe or matron in that English Jewry bore in his countenance one or more of these characteristics of his peerless Arab race.

"How beautiful they are!" mused CODLINGSBY, as he surveyed these placid groups calmly taking their pleasure in the sunset.

"D'you vant to look at a nishe coat?" a voice said, which made him start; and then some one behind him began handling a master-piece of STULTZ's with a familiarity which would have made the Baron tremble.

"RAFAEL MENDOZA!" exclaimed GODFREY.

"The same, LORD CODLINGSBY," the individual so apostrophised replied. "I told you we should meet again where you would little expect me. Will it please you to enter? this is Friday, and we close at sunset. It rejoices my heart to welcome you home." So saying RAFAEL laid his hand on his breast, and bowed, an Oriental reverence. All traces of the accent with which he first addressed LORD CODLINGSBY had vanished: it was a disguise; half the Hebrew's life is a disguise. He shields himself in craft, since the Norman boors persecuted him.

They passed under an awning of old clothes, tawdry fripperies, greasy spangles, and battered masks, into a shop as black and hideous as the entrance was foul. "*This* your home, RAFAEL?" said LORD CODLINGSBY.

"Why not?" RAFAEL answered. "I am tired of Schloss Schinkenstein; the Rhine bores me after a while. It is too hot for Florence; besides they have not completed the picture gallery, and my palace smells of putty. You wouldn't have a man, *mon cher*, bury himself in his château in Normandy, out of the hunting season? The Rugantino Palace stupifies me. Those Titians are so gloomy, I shall have my HOBBIMAS and TENIERS, I think, from my house at the Hague hung over them."

"How many castles, palaces, houses, warehouses,

shops, have you, RAFAEL?" LORD CODLINGSBY asked, laughing.

"This is one" RAFAEL answered. "Come in."

II.

THE noise in the old town was terrific; Great Tom was booming sullenly over the uproar; the bell of Saint Mary's was clanging with alarm; St. Giles's tocsin chimed furiously; howls, curses, flights of brickbats, stones shivering windows, groans of wounded men, cries of frightened females, cheers of either contending party as it charged the enemy from Carfax to Trumpington Street, proclaimed that the battle was at its height.

In Berlin they would have said it was a revolution, and the cuirassiers would have been charging, sabre in hand, amidst that infuriate mob. In France they would have brought down artillery, and played on it with twenty-four pounders. In Cambridge nobody heeded the disturbance—it was a Town and Gown row.

The row arose at a boat-race. The Town boat (manned by eight stout barges, with the redoubted RULLOCK for stroke) had bumped the Brazennose light oar, usually at the head of the river. High words arose regarding the dispute. After returning from Granchester, when the boats pulled back to

Christchurch meadows, the disturbance between the Townsmen and the University youths—their invariable opponents—grew louder and more violent, until it broke out in open battle. Sparring and skirmishing took place along the pleasant fields that lead from the University gate down to the broad and shining waters of the Cam, and under the walls of Baliol and Sidney Sussex. The Duke of Bellamont (then a dashing young sizar at Exeter) had a couple of rounds with Billy Butt, the bow oar of the Bargee boat. Vavasour of Brazennose was engaged with a powerful butcher, a well-known champion of the Town party, when, the great University bells ringing to dinner, truce was called between the combatants, and they retired to their several colleges for refection.

During the boat-race, a gentleman pulling in a canoe, and smoking a Nargilly, had attracted no ordinary attention. He rowed about a hundred yards ahead of the boats in the race, so that he could have a good view of that curious pastime. If the eight-oars neared him, with a few rapid strokes of his flashing paddles his boat shot a furlong ahead; then he would wait, surveying the race, and sending up volumes of odour from his cool Nargilly.

"Who is he?" asked the crowds who panted along the shore, encouraging, according to Cambridge wont, the efforts of the oarsmen in the race. Town and

Gown alike asked who it was, who, with an ease so provoking, in a barque so singular, with a form seemingly so slight, but a skill so prodigious, beat their best men. No answer could be given to the query, save that a gentleman in a dark travelling-chariot, preceded by six fourgons and a courier, had arrived the day before at the Hoop Inn, opposite Brazennose, and that the stranger of the canoe seemed to be the individual in question.

No wonder the boat, that all admired so, could compete with any that ever was wrought by Cambridge artificer or Putney workman. That boat—slim, shining, and shooting through the water like a pike after a small fish—was a caique from Tophana; it had distanced the Sultan's oarsmen, and the best crews of the Capitan Pasha in the Bosphorus; it was the workmanship of Togrul-Beg, Caikjee Bashee of his Highness. The Bashee had refused fifty thousand tomauns from Count Boutenieff, the Russian Ambassador, for that little marvel. When his head was taken off, the Father of Believers presented the boat to Rafael Mendoza.

It was Rafael Mendoza that saved the Turkish Monarchy after the battle of Nezeeb. By sending three millions of piastres to the Seraskier; by bribing Colonel de St. Cornichon, the French envoy in the camp of the victorious Ibrahim, the march of the Egyptian army was stopped—the menaced empire of the Ottomans was saved from ruin; the MARCHIONESS OF STOKEPOGIS, our Ambassador's lady, appeared in a suit of diamonds which outblazed even the Romanoff jewels, and RAFAEL MENDOZA obtained the little caique. He never travelled without it. It was scarcely heavier than an arm-chair. BARONI, the courier, had carried it down to the Cam that morning, and RAFAEL had seen the singular sport which we have mentioned.

The dinner over, the young men rushed from their colleges, flushed, full-fed, and eager for battle. If the Gown was angry, the Town, too, was on the alert. From Iffley and Barnwell, from factory and mill, from wharf and warehouse, the Town poured out to meet their enemy, and the battle was soon general. From the Addenbrook's hospital to the Blenheim turnpike, all Cambridge was in an uproar—the College gates closed—the shops barricaded—the shopboys away in support of their brother townsmen—the battle raged, and the Gown had the worst of the fight.

A luncheon of many courses had been provided for RAFAEL MENDOZA at his inn, but he smiled at the clumsy efforts of the University cooks to entertain him, and a couple of dates and a glass of water formed his meal. In vain the discomfited landlord pressed him to partake of the slighted banquet. "A breakfast! psha!" said he. "My good man, I have nineteen cooks, at salaries rising from four hundred a-year. I can have a dinner at any hour, but a Town and Gown row (a brickbat here flying through the window, crashed the caraffe of water in MENDOZA's hand)—a Town and Gown row is a novelty to me. The Town has the best of it, clearly, though the men outnumber the lads. Ha, a good blow! How that tall townsman went down before yonder slim young fellow in the scarlet trencher cap."

"That is the LORD CODLINGSBY," the landlord said.

"A light weight, but a pretty fighter," MENDOZA remarked. "Well hit with your left, LORD CODLINGSBY; well parried, LORD CODLINGSBY; claret drawn, by Jupiter!"

"Ours is werry fine," the landlord said. "Will your highness have Chateau Margaux or Laffitte?"

"He never can be going to match himself against that bargeman!" RAFAEL exclaimed, as an enormous boatman—no other than RULLOCK—indeed, the most famous bruiser of Cambridge, and before whose fists the gownsmen went down like ninepins, fought his way up to the spot where, with admirable spirit and resolution, LORD CODLINGSBY and one or two of his friends were making head against a number of the Town.

The young noble faced the huge champion with the gallantry of his race, but was no match for the enemy's strength, and weight, and sinew, and went down at every round. The brutal fellow had no mercy on the lad. His savage treatment chafed MENDOZA as he viewed the unequal combat from the inn-window. "Hold your hand!" he cried to this GOLIATH; "Don't you see he's but a boy?"

"Down he goes again!" the bargeman cried, not heeding the interruption. "Down he goes again: I likes wapping a Lord!"

"Coward!" shouted MENDOZA; and to fling open the window amidst a shower of brickbats, to vault over the balcony, to slide down one of the pillars to the ground, was an instant's work.

At the next he stood before the enormous bargeman.

* * * * *

After the Coroner's Inquest, MENDOZA gave ten thousand pounds to each of the bargeman's ten children, and it was thus his first acquaintance was formed with LORD CODLINGSBY.

But we are lingering on the threshold of the house in Holywell Street. Let us go in!

III.

GODFREY and RAFAEL passed from the street into the outer shop of the old mansion in Holywell Street. It was a masquerade warehouse, to all appearance.

A dark-eyed damsel of the nation was standing at the dark and grimy counter, strewed with old feathers, old yellow boots, old stage mantles, painted masks, blind and yet gazing at you with a look of sad death-like intelligence from the vacancy behind their sockets.

A medical student was trying one of the doublets of orange-tawney and silver, slashed with dirty light blue. He was going to a masquerade that night. He thought POLLY PATTENS would admire him in the dress—POLLY PATTENS, the fairest of maids-of-all-work—the Borough VENUS, adored by half the youth of GUY'S.

"You look like a Prince in it, MR. LINT," pretty RACHEL said, coaxing him with her beady black eyes.

"It *is* the cheese," replied MR. LINT; "it ain't the dress that don't suit, my rose of Sharon; it's the *figure*. Hullo, RAFAEL, is that you, my lad of sealing wax? Come and intercede for me with this wild gazelle; she says I can't have it under fifteen bob for the night. And it's too much: cuss me if it's not too much, unless you'll take my little bill at two months, RAFAEL."

"There's a sweet pretty brigand's dress you may have for half de monish," RAFAEL replied; "there's a splendid clown for eight bob; but for dat Spanish dress, selp ma MOSHESH, MISTRAER LINT, ve'd ask a guinea of any but you. Here's a gentlemansh just come to look at it. Look ear, MR. BROWNSH, did you ever shee a nisher ting dan dat?" So saying, RAFAEL turned to LORD CODLINGSBY with the utmost gravity, and displayed to him the garment about which the young Medicus was haggling.

"Cheap at the money," CODLINGSBY replied; "if you won't make up your mind, sir, I should like to engage it myself." But the thought that another should appear before POLLY PATTENS in that costume was too much for MR. LINT: he agreed to pay the fifteen shillings for the garment. And RAFAEL, pocketing the money with perfect simplicity, said "Dis vay, MR. BROWNSH; dere's someting vill shoot you in the next shop."

LORD CODLINGSBY followed him, wondering.

"You are surprised at our system," said RAFAEL, marking the evident bewilderment of his friend. "Confess you would call it meanness—my huxtering with yonder young fool. I call it simplicity. Why throw away a shilling without need? Our race never did. A shilling is four men's bread: shall I disdain to defile my fingers by holding them out relief in their necessity? It is you who are mean—you Normans—not we of the ancient race. You have your vulgar measurement for great things and small. You call a thousand pounds respectable, and a shekel despicable. Psha, my CODLINGSBY! One is as the other.

I trade in pennies and in millions. I am above or below neither."

They were passing through a second shop, smelling strongly of cedar, and, in fact, piled up with bales of those pencils which the young Hebrews are in the habit of vending through the streets. "I have sold bundles and bundles of these," said RAFAEL. "My little brother is now out with oranges in Piccadilly. I am bringing him up to be head of our house at Amsterdam. We all do it. I had myself to see ROTHSCHILD in Eaton Place, this morning, about the Irish loan, of which I have taken three millions; and as I wanted to walk, I carried the bag.

"You should have seen the astonishment of LAUDA LATYMER, the ARCHBISHOP OF CROYDON'S daughter, as she was passing to St. Bennet's, Knightsbridge, and as she fancied she recognised in the man who was crying old clothes the gentleman with whom she had talked at the COUNT DE SAINT AULAIRE'S the night before." Something like a blush flushed over the pale features of MENDOZA as he mentioned the LADY LAUDA'S name. "Come on," said he. They passed through various warehouses—the orange room, the sealing-wax room, the six-bladed-knife department, and finally came to an old baize door. RAFAEL opened the baized door by some secret contrivance, and they were in a black passage, with a curtain at the end.

He clapped his hands; the curtain at the end of the passage drew back, and a flood of golden light streamed on the Hebrew and his visitor.

CHAPTER XXIV.

They entered a moderate-sized apartment—indeed, Holywell Street is not above a hundred yards long, and this chamber was not more than half that length—and fitted up with the simple taste of its owner.

The carpet was of white velvet—(laid over several webs of Aubusson, Ispahan, and Axminster, so that your foot gave no more sound as it trod upon the yielding plain than the shadow did which followed you)—of white velvet, painted with flowers, arabesques, and classic figures, by Sir William Ross, J. M. Turner, R. A., Mrs. Mee, and Paul Delaroche. The edges were wrought with seed-pearls, and fringed with Valenciennes lace and bullion. The walls were hung with cloth of silver, embroidered with gold figures, over which were worked pomegranates, polyanthuses, and passion-flowers, in ruby, amethyst, and smaragd. The drops of dew which the artificer had sprinkled on the flowers were diamonds. The hangings were overhung by pictures yet more costly. Giorgione the gorgeous, Titian the golden,

RUBENS the ruddy and pulpy (the PAN of Painting), some of MURILLO's beatified shepherdesses, who smile on you out of darkness like a star; a few score first-class LEONARDOS, and fifty of the master-pieces of the patron of JULIUS and LEO, the Imperial genius of URBINO, covered the walls of the little chamber. Divans of carved amber covered with ermine went round the room, and in the midst was a fountain, pattering and babbling with jets of double-distilled otto of roses.

"Pipes, GOLIATH!" RAFAEL said gaily to a little negro with a silver collar (he spoke to him in his native tongue of Dongola); "and welcome to our snuggery, my CODLINGSBY. We are quieter here than in the front of the house, and I wanted to show you a picture. I'm proud of my pictures. That LEONARDO came from Genoa, and was a gift to our father from my cousin, MARSHAL MANASSEH; that MURILLO was pawned to my uncle by MARIE ANTOINETTE before the flight to Varennes—the poor lady could not redeem the pledge, you know, and the picture remains with us. As for the RAFAEL, I suppose you are aware that he was one of our people. But what are you gazing at? O! my sister—I forgot—MIRIAM! this is the LORD CODLINGSBY."

She had been seated at an ivory piano-forte on a mother-of-pearl music-stool, trying a sonata of HERZ.

She rose when thus apostrophised. MIRIAM DE MENDOZA rose and greeted the stranger.

The Talmud relates that ADAM had two wives—ZILLAH the dark beauty; EVA the fair one. The ringlets of ZILLAH were black; those of EVA were golden. The eyes of ZILLAH were night; those of EVA were morning. CODLINGSBY was fair—of the fair Saxon race of HENGIST and HORSA—they called him MISS CODLINGSBY at school; but how much fairer was MIRIAM the Hebrew!

Her hair had that deep glowing tinge in it which has been the delight of all painters, and which, therefore, the vulgar sneer at. It was of burning auburn. Meandering over her fairest shoulders in twenty thousand minute ringlets, it hung to her waist and below it. A light blue velvet fillet clasped with a diamond aigrette, (valued at two hundred thousand tomauns, and bought from LIEUTENANT VICOVICH, who had received it from DOST MAHOMED,) with a simple bird of paradise formed her head gear. A sea-green cymar with short sleeves, displayed her exquisitely moulded arms to perfection, and was fastened by a girdle of emeralds over a yellow satin frock. Pink gauze trousers spangled with silver, and slippers of the same colour as the band which clasped her ringlets (but so covered with pearls that the original hue of the charming little papoosh disappeared entirely) completed her costume. She had three necklaces on, each of which would have dowered a Princess—her fingers glistened with rings to their rosy tips, and priceless bracelets, bangles, and armlets wound round an arm that was whiter than the ivory grand piano on which it leaned.

As MIRIAM DE MENDOZA greeted the stranger, turning upon him the solemn welcome of her eyes, CODLINGSBY swooned almost in the brightness of her beauty. It was well she spoke; the sweet kind voice restored him to consciousness. Muttering a few words of incoherent recognition, he sank upon a sandal-wood settee, as GOLIATH, the little slave, brought aromatic coffee in cups of opal, and alabaster spittoons, and pipes of the fragrant Gibelly.

"Mylord's pipe is out," said MIRIAM with a smile, remarking the bewilderment of her guest—who in truth forgot to smoke—and taking up a thousand pound note from a bundle on the piano, she lighted it at the taper and proceeded to re-illume the extinguished chibouk of LORD CODLINGSBY.

IV.

WHEN MIRIAM, returning to the mother-of-pearl music-stool, at a signal from her brother, touched the silver and enamelled keys of the ivory piano, and began to sing, LORD CODLINGSBY felt as if he were listening at the gates of Paradise, or were hearing JENNY LIND.

"LIND is a name of the Hebrew race; so is MENDELSSOHN, the Son of Almonds; so is ROSENTHAL, the Valley of the Roses; so is LÖWE or LEWIS or LYONS or LION—the beautiful and the brave alike give cognizances to the ancient people—you Saxons call yourselves BROWN, or SMITH, or RODGERS," RAFAEL observed to his friend; and, drawing the instrument from his pocket, he accompanied his sister, in the most ravishing manner, on a little gold and jewelled harp, of the kind peculiar to his nation.

All the airs which the Hebrew maid selected were written by composers of her race; it was either a hymn by ROSSINI, a polacca by BRAHAM, a delicious romance by SLOMAN, or a melody by WEBER, that, thrilling on the strings of the instrument, wakened a harmony on the fibres of the heart; but she sang no other than the songs of her nation.

"Beautiful one! sing ever, sing always," CODLINGSBY thought. "I could sit at thy feet as under a green palm-tree, and fancy that Paradise-birds were singing in the boughs."

RAFAEL read his thoughts. "We have Saxon blood too in our veins," he said. "You smile; but it is even so. An ancestress of ours made a *mésalliance* in the reign of your KING JOHN. Her name was REBECCA, daughter of ISAAC OF YORK, and she married in Spain, whither she had fled to the Court of KING BOABDIL, SIR WILFRID OF IVANHOE, then a widower by the demise of his first lady, ROWENA. The match was deemed a cruel insult amongst our people; but WILFRID conformed, and was a Rabbi of some note at the synagogue at Cordova. We are descended from him lineally. It is the only blot upon the escutcheon of the MENDOZAS."

As they sate talking together, the music finished, and MIRIAM having retired (though her song and her beauty were still present to the soul of the stranger) at a signal from MENDOZA, various messengers from the outer apartments came in to transact business with him.

First it was MR. AMINIDAB, who kissed his foot, and brought papers to sign. "How is the house in Grosvenor Square, AMINIDAB; and is your son tired of his yacht yet?" MENDOZA asked. "That is my twenty-fourth cashier," said RAFAEL to CODLINGSBY, when the obsequious clerk went away. "He is fond of display, and all my people may have what money they like."

Entered presently the LORD BAREACRES, on the affair of his mortgage. The LORD BAREACRES, strutting into the apartment with a haughty air, shrank back, nevertheless, with surprise on beholding the magnificence around him. "Little MORDECAI," said RAFAEL to a little orange-boy, who came in at the heels of the noble, "take this gentleman out and let him have ten thousand pounds. I can't do more for you, my lord, than this—I'm busy. Good bye!" and RAFAEL waved his hand to the peer, and fell to smoking his Nargilly.

A man with a square face, cat-like eyes, and a yellow moustache, came next. He had an hour-glass of a waist, and walked uneasily upon his high-heeled boots. "Tell your master that he shall have two millions more, but not another shilling," RAFAEL said. "That story about the five-and-twenty millions of ready money at Cronstadt is all bosh. They won't believe it in Europe. You understand me, Count GROGOMOFFSKI?"

"But his Imperial Majesty said four millions, and I shall get the knout unless—"

"Go and speak to MR. SHADRACH, in room Z 94, the fourth Court," said MENDOZA good-naturedly. "Leave me at peace, Count; don't you see it is Friday, and almost sunset?" The Calmuck envoy retired cringing, and left an odour of musk and candle-grease behind him.

An orange-man; an emissary from LOLA MONTES; a dealer in piping bulfinches; and a Cardinal in disguise, with a proposal for a new loan for the Pope, were heard by turns, and each, after a rapid colloquy in his own language, was dismissed by RAFAEL.

"The QUEEN must come back from Aranjuez, or

that king must be disposed of," RAFAEL exclaimed, as a yellow-faced ambassador from Spain, GENERAL THE DUKE OF OLLA PODRIDA, left him. "Which shall it be, my CODLINGSBY?" CODLINGSBY was about laughingly to answer, for indeed he was amazed to find all the affairs of the world represented here, and Holywell Street the centre of Europe, when three knocks of a peculiar nature were heard, and MENDOZA, starting up, said, "Ha! there are only four men in the world who know that signal." At once, and with a reverence quite distinct from his former *nonchalant* manner, he advanced towards the new comer.

He was an old man—an old man evidently, too, of the Hebrew race—the light of his eyes was unfathomable—about his mouth there played an inscrutable smile. He had a cotton umbrella, and old trowsers, and old boots, and an old wig, curling at the top like a rotten old pear.

He sate down as if tired, in the first seat at hand, as RAFAEL made him the lowliest reverence.

"I am tired," says he; "I have come in fifteen hours. I am ill at Neuilly," he added with a grin. "Get me some *eau sucrée*, and tell me the news, PRINCE DE MENDOZA. These bread rows; this unpopularity of GUIZOT; this odious Spanish conspiracy against my darling MONTPENSIER and daughter; this ferocity of PALMERSTON against COLETTI, make me quite ill. Give me your opinion, my dear duke. But ha! whom have we here?"

The august individual who had spoken, had used the Hebrew language to address MENDOZA, and the LORD CODLINGSBY might easily have pleaded ignorance of that tongue. But he had been at Cambridge, where all the youth acquire it perfectly.

"*Sire*," said he, "I will not disguise from you that I know the ancient tongue in which you speak. There are probably secrets between MENDOZA and your MAJ—"

"Hush!" said RAFAEL, leading him from the room: "*Au revoir*, dear CODLINGSBY. His Majesty is one of *us*," he whispered at the door; "so is the Pope of Rome; so is * * *"—a whisper concealed the rest.

"Gracious powers! is it so?" said CODLINGSBY, musing. He entered into Holywell Street. The sun was sinking.

"It is time," said he, "to go and fetch FIFINE to the Olympic."

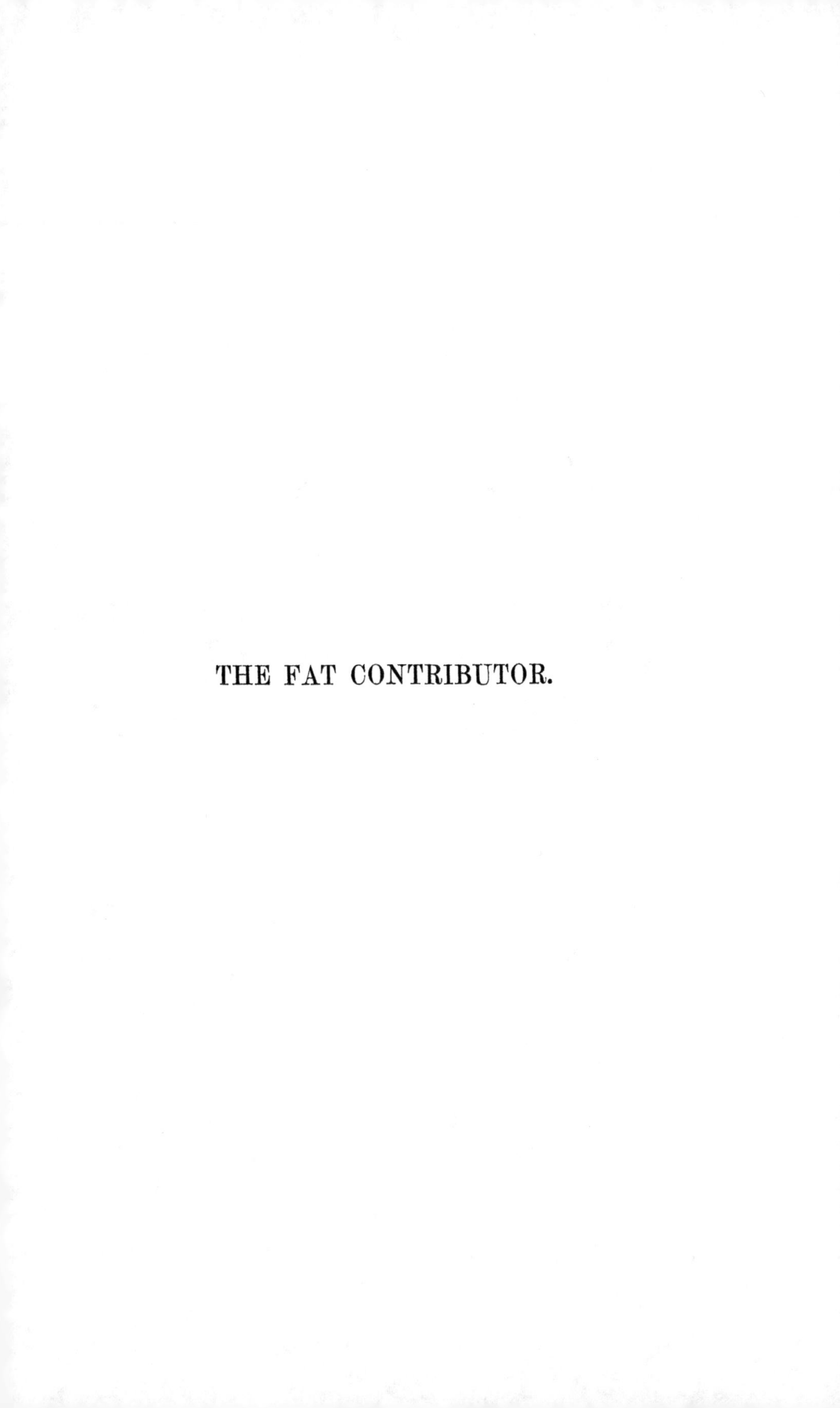

THE FAT CONTRIBUTOR.

BRIGHTON.

BY THE FAT CONTRIBUTOR.

As there are some consumptive travellers, who, by dodging about to Italy, to Malta, to Madeira, manage to cheat the winter, and for whose lungs a perpetual warmth is necessary; so there are people to whom, in like manner, London is a necessity of existence, and who follow it all the year round. Such individuals, when London goes out of town, follow it to Brighton, which is, at this season, London *plus* prawns for breakfast and the sea-air. Blessings on the sea-air, which gives you an appetite to eat them!

You may get a decent bed-room and sitting-room here for a guinea a day. Our friends the BOTIBOLS have three rooms, and a bedstead disguised like a chest of drawers in the drawing-room, for which they pay something less than a hundred pounds a month. I could not understand last night why the old gentleman, who usually goes to bed early, kept yawning and fidgetting in the drawing-room after tea; until, with some hesitation, he made the confession that the apartment in question was his bed-room, and revealed the mystery of the artful chest of drawers. BOTIBOL'S house in Bedford Square is as spacious as an Italian palace: the second-floor front, in which the worthy man sleeps, would accommodate a regiment, and here they squeeze him into a *chiffonnière!* How MRS. B. and the four delightful girls can be stowed away in the back room, I tremble to think: what bachelor has a right to ask? But the air of the sea makes up for the closeness of the lodgings. I have just seen them on the Cliff—mother and daughters were all blooming like crimson double dahlias!

You meet everybody on that Cliff. For a small charge you may hire the very fly in which I rode; with the very horse, and the very postilion, in a pink striped chintz jacket—which may have been the cover of an arm-chair once—and straight whitey-brown hair, and little wash-leather inexpressibles, the cheapest little caricature of a post-boy eyes have ever lighted on. I seldom used to select his carriage, for the horse and vehicle looked feeble, and unequal to bearing a person of weight; but, last Sunday, I saw an Israelitish family of distinction ensconced in the poor little carriage—the ladies with the most flaming polkas, and flounces all the way up; the gent, in velvet waistcoat, with pins in his breast big enough once to have surmounted the door of his native pawnbroker's shop, and a complement of hook-nosed children, magnificent in attire. Their number and magnificence did not break the carriage down; the little postilion bumped up and down as usual, as the old horse went his usual pace. How they spread out, and basked, and shone, and were happy in the sun there — those honest people! The Mosaic Arabs abound here; and they rejoice and are idle with a grave and solemn pleasure, as becomes their Eastern origin.

If you don't mind the expense, hire a ground-floor window on the Cliff, and examine the stream of human nature which passes by. That stream is a league in length; it pours from Brunswick Terrace to Kemp Town, and then tumbles back again; and so rolls, and as it rolls perpetually, keeps rolling on from three o'clock till dinner-time.

Ha! what a crowd of well-known London faces you behold here—only the sallow countenances look pink now, and devoid of care. I have seen this very day, at least—

Forty-nine Railroad directors, who would have been at Baden-Baden but for the lines in progress; and who, though breathing the fresh air, are within an hour and a half of the City.

Thirteen barristers, of more or less repute, including the SOLICITOR-GENERAL himself, whose open and jovial countenance beamed with benevolence upon the cheerful scene.

A Hebrew dentist driving a curricle.

At least twelve well-known actors or actresses. It went to my heart to see the most fashionable of them, driving about in a little four-wheeled pony-chaise, the like of which might be hired for five shillings.

Then you have tight-laced dragoons, trotting up and down with solemn, handsome, stupid faces, and huge yellow mustachios. Myriads of flies, laden with happy cockneys; pathetic invalid chairs trail along, looking too much like coffins already, in which poor people are brought out to catch a glimpse of the sun. Grand equipages are scarce; I saw LADY WILHELMINA WIGGINS's lovely nose and auburn ringlets peeping out of a cab, hired at half-a-crown an hour, between her ladyship and her sister, the PRINCESS OYSTEROWSKI.

* * * * *

The old gentleman who began to take lessons when we were here three years ago, at the Tepid Swimming Bath, with the conical top, I am given to understand is still there, and may be seen in the water, from nine till five.

MEDITATIONS OVER BRIGHTON.

BY "PUNCH'S" COMMISSIONER.

(From the Devil's Dyke.)

When the exultant and long-eared animal described in the fable revelled madly in the frog-pond, dashing about his tail and hoof among the unfortunate inhabitants of that piece of water, it is stated, that the frogs remonstrated, exclaiming, "Why, O donkey, do you come kicking about in our habitation? It may be good fun to you to lash out, and plunge, and kick in this absurd manner, but it is death to us;" on which the good-natured quadruped agreed to discontinue his gambols; and left the frogs to bury their dead and rest henceforth undisturbed in their pool.

The inhabitants of Brighton are the frogs—and I dare say they will agree as to the applicability of the rest of the simile. It might be good fun to *me* to "mark their manners, and their ways survey;" but could it be altogether agreeable to them? I am sorry to confess it has not proved so, having received at least three hundred letters of pathetic remonstrance, furious complaint, angry swagger, and threatening omens, entreating me to leave the Brightonians alone. The lodging-house keepers are up in arms. MRS. SCREW says *she* never let her lodgings at a guinea a day, and invites me to occupy her drawing and bed-room for five guineas a week. MR. SQUEEZER swears that a guinea a day is an atrocious calumny: he would turn his wife, his children, and his bed-ridden mother in-law out of doors if he could get such a sum for the rooms they occupy—(but this, I suspect is a pretext of SQUEEZER'S to get rid of his mother-in-law, in which project I wish him luck). MRS. SLOP hopes she may never again cut a slice out of a lodger's joint (the cannibal!) if she won't be ready at the most crowdidest of seasons to let her first-floor for six pounds: and finally, MR. SKIVER writes: —"Sir,—your-ill advised publication has passed like a whirlwind over the lodging-houses of Brighton. You have rendered our families desolate, and prematurely closed our season. As you have destroyed the lodging-houses, couldn't you, now, walk into the boarding houses, and say a kind word to ruin the hotels?"

And is it so? Is the power of the Commissioner's eye so fatal that it withers the object on which it falls? Is the condition of his life so dreadful that he destroys all whom he comes near? Have I made a post-boy wretched—five thousand lodging-house-keepers furious—twenty thousand Jews unhappy? If so, and I really possess a power so terrible, I had best come out in the tragic line.

I went, pursuant to orders, to the Swiss Cottage, at Shoreham, where the first object that struck my eye was a scene, in the green lake there, which I am credibly informed is made of pea-soup: two honest girls were rowing about their friend on this enchanting water. There was a cloudless sky overhead—rich treats were advertised for the six frequenters of the gardens; a variety of entertainments was announced in the Hall of Amusement.—Mr. and Mrs. Aminadab (here, too, the Hebrews have penetrated) were advertised as about to sing some of their most favourite comic songs and * * * * *

But *no*, I will *not* describe the place. Why should my fatal glance bring a curse upon it? The pea-soup lake would dry up—leaving its bed a vacant tureen—the leaves would drop from the scorched trees—the pretty flowers would wither and fade—the rockets would not rise at night, nor the rebel wheels go round—the money-taker at the door would grow mouldy and die in his moss-grown and deserted cell. —Aminadab would lose his engagement. Why should these things be, and this ruin occur? James! pack the portmanteau and tell the landlord to bring the bill; order horses immediately—this day I will quit Brighton.

Other appalling facts have come to notice: all showing more or less the excitement created by my publication.

The officers of the 150th Hussars, accused of looking handsome, solemn, and stupid, have had a meeting in the mess-room, where the two final epithets have been rescinded in a string of resolutions.

But it is the poor yellow-breeched postilion who has most suffered. When the picture of him came out, crowds flocked to see him. He was mobbed all the way down the Cliff; wherever he drove his little phaëton, people laughed, and pointed with the finger and said, "That is he." The poor child was thus made the subject of public laughter by my interference—and what has been the consequence? In order to disguise him as much as possible, *his Master has bought him a hat.*

The children of Israel are in a fury too. They do not like to ride in flies since my masterly representation of them a fortnight since. They are giving up their houses daily. You read in the Brighton papers, among the departures, "—— NEBUZARADAN, Esq., and family for London;" or SOLOMON RAMOTH-GILEAD, Esq., has quitted his mansion in Marine Crescent; circumstances having induced him to shorten his stay among us," and so on. The people emigrate by hundreds; they can't bear to be made the object of remark in the public walks and drives—and they are flying from a city of which they might have made a new Jerusalem.

A BRIGHTON NIGHT ENTERTAINMENT.

BY PUNCH'S COMMISSIONER.

I HAVE always had a taste for the second-rate in life. Second-rate poetry, for instance, is an uncommon deal pleasanter to my fancy than your great thundering first-rate epic poems. Your MILTONS and DANTES are magnificent,—but a bore: whereas an ode of HORACE, or a song of TOMMY MOORE, is always fresh, sparkling, and welcome. Second-rate claret, again, is notoriously better than first-rate wine: you get the former genuine, whereas the latter is a loaded and artificial composition that cloys the palate and bothers the reason.

Second-rate beauty in women is likewise, I maintain, more agreeable than first-rate charms. Your first-rate Beauty is grand, severe, awful—a faultless, frigid angel of five feet nine—superb to behold at church, or in the park, or at a drawing-room—but ah! how inferior to a sweet little second-rate creature, with smiling eyes, and a little second-rate *nez retroussé*, with which you fall in love in a minute.

Second-rate novels I also assert to be superior to the best works of fiction. They give you no trouble to read, excite no painful emotions—you go through them with a gentle, languid, agreeable interest. Mr. James's romances are perfect in this way. The *ne plus ultra* of indolence may be enjoyed during their perusal.

For the same reason, I like second-rate theatrical entertainments—a good little company in a provincial town, acting good old stupid stock comedies and farces; where nobody comes to the theatre, and you may lie at ease in the pit, and get a sort of intimacy with each actor and actress, and know every bar of the music that the three or four fiddlers of the little orchestra play throughout the season.

The Brighton Theatre would be admirable but for one thing—Mr. Hooper, the Manager, will persist in having Stars down from London—blazing Macreadys, resplendent Miss Cushmans, fiery Wallacks, and the like. On these occasions it is very possible that the house may be filled and the Manager's purpose answered; but where does all your comfort go then? You can't loll over four benches in the pit—you are squeezed and hustled in an inconvenient crowd there—you are fatigued by the perpetual struggles of the apple-and-ginger-beer boy, who *will* pass down your row—and for what do you undergo this labour? To see *Hamlet* and *Lady Mac-*

beth, forsooth ! as if every body had not seen them a thousand times. No, on such star nights " The Commissioner" prefers a walk on the Cliff to the charms of the Brighton Theatre. I can have first-rate tragedy in London: in the country give me good old country fare—the good old comedies and farces—the dear good old melodramas.

We had one the other day in perfection. We were, I think, about four of us in the pit; the ginger-beer boy might wander about quite at his ease. There was a respectable family in a private box, and some pleasant fellows in the gallery; and we saw, with leisure and delectation, that famous old melodrama, *The Warlock of the Glen.*

In a pasteboard cottage, on the banks of the Atlantic Ocean, there lived once a fisherman, who had a little canvass boat, in which it is a wonder he was never swamped, for the boat was not above three feet long; and I was astonished at his dwelling in the cottage, too; for, though a two-storied one, it was not above five feet high; and I am sure the fisherman was six feet without his shoes.

As he was standing at the door of his cot, looking at some young persons of the neighbourhood who were dancing a reel, a scream was heard, as issuing from the neighbouring forest, and a lady with dishevelled hair, and a beautiful infant in her hand, rushed in. What meant that scream? We were longing to know, but the gallery insisted on the reel over again, and the poor injured lady had to wait until the dance was done before she could explain her unfortunate case.

It was briefly this: she was no other than *Adela, Countess of Glencairn;* the boy in her hand was *Glencairn's* only child: three years since her gallant husband had fallen in fight, or, worse still, by the hand of the assassin.

He had left a brother, *Clanronald.* What was the conduct of that surviving relative? Was it fraternal towards the widowed *Adela?* Was it avuncular to the orphan boy? Ah, no! For three years he had locked her up in his castle, under pretence that she was mad, pursuing her all the while with his odious addresses. But she loathed his suit; and, refusing to become *Mrs.* (or *Lady*) *Clanronald*, took this opportunity to escape and fling herself on the protection of the loyal vassals of her lord.

She had hardly told her pathetic tale when voices were heard without. Cries of "Follow! follow!" resounded through the wildwood; the gentlemen and ladies engaged in the reel fled, and the Countess and her child, stepping into the skiff, disappeared down a slote, to the rage and disappointment of *Clanronald*, who now arrived—a savage-looking nobleman indeed! and followed by two ruffians, of most ferocious aspect, and having in their girdles a pair of those little notched dumpy swords, with round iron hilts to guard the knuckles, by which I knew that a combat would probably take place ere long. And the result proved that I was right.

Flying along the wild margent of the sea, in the next act, the poor *Adela* was pursued by *Clanronald;* but though she jumped into the waves to avoid him, the unhappy lady was rescued from the briny element, and carried back to her prison; *Clanronald* swearing a dreadful oath that she should marry him that very day.

He meanwhile gave orders to his two ruffians, *Murdoch* and *Hamish*, to pursue the little boy into the wood, and there—there *murder* him.

But there is always a power in melodramas that watches over innocence; and these two wretched ones were protected by THE WARLOCK OF THE GLEN.

All through their misfortunes, this mysterious being watched them with a tender interest. When the two ruffians were about to murder the child, he and the fisherman rescued him—their battle swords (after a brief combat of four) sank powerless before his wizard staff, and they fled in terror.

Haste we to the Castle of Glencairn. What ceremony is about to take place? What has assembled those two noblemen, and those three ladies in calico trains? A marriage! But what a union! The lady *Adela* is dragged to the chapel-door by the trusculent

Clanronald. "Lady," he says, "you are mine. Resistance is unavailing. Submit with good grace. Henceforth, what power on earth can separate you from me?"

"MINE CAN," cries the *Warlock of the Glen*, rushing in. "Tyrant and assassin of thy brother! know that Glencairn—Glencairn, thy brother and Lord, whom thy bravos were commissioned to slay—know that, for three years, a solemn vow (sworn to the villain that spared his life, and expired yesterday) bound him never to reveal his existence—know that he is near at hand; and repent, while yet there is time."

The lady *Adela's* emotion may be guessed when she heard this news: but *Clanronald*, received it with contemptuous scepticism. "And where *is* this dead man come alive?" laughed he.

"He is HERE," shouted the *Warlock of the Glen:* and to fling away his staff—to dash off his sham beard and black gown—to appear in a red dress, with tights and yellow boots, as became Glencairn's earl—was the work of a moment. The Countess recognized him with a scream of joy. *Clanronald* retired, led off by two soldiers; and the joy of the Earl and Countess was completed by the arrival of their only son (a clever little girl of the Hebrew persuasion) in the arms of the fisherman.

The curtain fell on this happy scene. The fiddlers had ere this disappeared. The ginger-beer boy went home to a virtuous family, that was probably looking out for him. The respectable family in the boxes went off in a fly. The little audience spread abroad, and were lost in the labyrinths of the city. The lamps of the Theatre Royal were extinguished: and all—all was still.

BRIGHTON IN 1847.

BY THE F. C.

I.

Have the kindness, my dear Pugsby, to despatch me a line when they have done painting the smoking-room at the Megatherium, that I may come back to town. After suffering as we have all the year, not so much from the bad ventilation of the room, as from the suffocating dulness of Wheezer, Snoozer, and Whiffler, who frequent it, I had hoped for quiet by the sea-shore here, and that our three abominable acquaintances had quitted England.

I had scarcely been ten minutes in the place, my ever dear Pugsby, when I met old Snoozer walking with young De Bosky, of the Tatters-and-Starvation Club, on the opposite side of our square, and ogling the girls on the Cliff, the old wretch, as if he had not a wife and half-a-dozen daughters of his own, in Pocklington Square. He hooked on to my arm as if he had been the Old Man of the Sea, and I found myself introduced to young De Bosky, a man whom

I have carefully avoided as an odious and disreputable tiger, the tuft on whose chin has been always particularly disagreeable to me, and who is besides a Captain, or Commodore, or some such thing, in the Bundelcund Cavalry. The clink and glitter of his spurs is perfectly abominable: he is screwed so tight in his waistband that I wish it could render him speechless (for when he *does* speak he is so stupid that he sends you to sleep while actually walking with him); and as for his chest, which he bulges out against the shoulders of all the passers-by, I am sure that he carries a part of his wardrobe in it, and that he is wadded with stockings and linen as if he were a walking carpet-bag.

This fellow saluted two-thirds of the carriages which passed, with a knowing nod, and a military swagger so arrogant, that I feel continually the greatest desire to throttle him.

Well, Sir, before we had got from the Tepid Swimming Bath to Mutton's the pastrycook's, whom should we meet but Wheezer, to be sure. Wheezer, driving up and down the Cliff at half-a-crown an hour, with his hideous family, Mrs. Wheezer, the Miss Wheezers in fur tippets and drawn bonnets with spring-flowers in them, a huddle and squeeze of little Wheezers sprawling and struggling on the back seat of the carriage, and that horrible boy whom Wheezer brings to the Club sometimes, actually seated on the box of the fly, and ready to drive, if the coachman should be intoxicated or inclined to relinquish his duty.

WHEEZER sprang out of the vehicle with a cordiality that made me shudder. "Hullo, my boy!" said he, seizing my trembling hand. "What! *you* here? Hang me if the whole Club isn't here. I'm at 56, Horse Marine Parade. Where are you lodging? We're out for a holiday, and will make a jolly time of it."

The benighted, the conceited old wretch! He would not let go my hand until I told him where I resided—at MRS. MUGGERIDGE's in Black Lion Street, where I have a tolerable view of the sea, if I risk the loss of my equilibrium and the breakage of my back, by stretching three quarters of my body out of my drawing-room window.

As he stopped to speak to me, his carriage of course stopped likewise, forcing all the vehicles in front and behind him, to halt or to precipitate themselves over the railings on to the shingles and the sea. The cabs, the flys, the shandrydans, the sedan-chairs with the poor old invalids inside; the old maids', the dowagers' chariots, out of which you see countenances scarcely less deathlike; the stupendous cabs, out of which the whiskered heroes of the gallant Onety-oneth look down on us people on foot; the hacks mounted by young ladies from the equestrian schools, by whose sides the riding-masters canter confidentially—everybody stopped. There was a perfect strangury in the street; and I should have liked not only to throttle DE BOSKY, but to massacre WHEEZER, too.

The wretched though unconscious being insisted on nailing me for dinner before he would leave me; and I heard him say (that is, by the expression of his countenance, and the glances which his wife and children cast at me, I *knew* he said), "That is the young and dashing FOLKSTONE CANTERBURY, the celebrated contributor to *Punch.*"

The crowd, Sir, on the Cliff was perfectly frightful. It is my belief nobody goes abroad any more. Everybody is at Brighton. I met three hundred at least of our acquaintances in the course of a quarter of an hour, and before we could reach Brunswick Square I met dandies, City men, Members of Parliament. I met my tailor walking with his wife, with a geranium blooming in his wretched button-hole, as if money wasn't tight in the City, and everybody had paid him everything everybody owed him. I turned and sickened at the sight of that man. "SNOOZER," said I, "I will go on the Pier."

I went, and to find what?—WHIFFLER, by all that is unmerciful!—WHIFFLER, whom we see every day, in the same chair, at the Megatherium. WHIFFLER, whom not to see is to make all the good fellows at the Club happy. I have seen him every day, and many times a day since. At the moment of our first rencontre I was so *saisi*, so utterly overcome by rage and despair, that I would have flung myself into the azure waves sparkling calmly around me, but for the chains of the Pier.

I did not take that aqueous suicidal plunge—I resolved to live, and why, my dear PUGSBY? Who do you think approached us? Were you not at one of his parties last season? I have polked in his saloons, I have nestled under the mahogany of his dining-room, at least one hundred and twenty thousand times. It was MR. GOLDMORE, the East India Director, with MRS. G. on his arm, and—oh, Heavens! —FLORENCE and VIOLET GOLDMORE, with pink parasols, walking behind their parents!

"What, *you* here?" said the good and hospitable man, holding out his hand, and giving a slap on the boards (or deck I may say) with his bamboo, "hang it, every one's here. Come and dine at seven. Brunswick Square."

I looked in VIOLET's eyes. FLORENCE is rather an old bird, and wears spectacles, so that looking in *her* eyes is out of the question. I looked in VIOLET's eyes, and said I'd come with the greatest pleasure.

"As for you, DE BOSKY"—(I forget whether I mentioned that the whiskered Bundelcund buck had come with me on to the Pier, whither SNOOZER would not follow us, declining to pay the twopence)—"as for *you*, De Bosky, you may come, or not, as you like."

"Won't I," said he, grinning, with a dandified Bundelcund nod, and wagging his odious head.

I could have wrenched it off and flung it to the ocean. But I restrained my propensity, and we agreed, that, for the sake of economy, we would go to Mr. Goldmore's in the same fly.

II.

The very first spoonful of the clear soup at the Director's, told me that my excellent friend Paradol (the *chef* who came to Mr. Goldmore, Portland Place, when Gottlebury House was shut up by the lamented levanting of the noble Earl) was established among the furnaces below. A clear, brown soup—none of your filthy, spiced, English hell-broths, but light, brisk, and delicate—always sets me off for the evening: it invigorates and enlivens me, my dear Pugsby: I give you my honour it does—and when I am in a *good* humour, I am, I flatter myself—what shall I say?—well, *not disagreeable.*

On this day, Sir, I was delightful. Although that booby De Bosky conducted Miss Violet Goldmore down stairs, yet the wretch, absorbed in his victuals, and naturally of an unutterable dulness, did not make a single remark during the dinner, whereas

I literally blazed with wit. Sir, I even made one of the footmen laugh—a perilous joke for the poor fellow, who, I dare say, will be turned off in consequence. I talked sentiment to FLORENCE (women in spectacles are almost always sentimental); cookery to SIR HARCOURT GULPH, who particularly asked my address, and I have no doubt intends to invite me to his dinners in town; military affairs with MAJOR BANGLES of the Onety-oneth Hussars, who was with the regiment at Aliwal and Ferozeshah, and drives about a prodigious cab at Brighton, with a captured Sikh behind, disguised as a tiger; to MRS. GOLDMORE I abused LADY TODDLE-ROWDY'S new carriages and absurd appearance (she is seventy-four, if she is a day, and she wears a white muslin frock and frilled trowsers, with a wig curling down her old back, and I do believe puts on a pinafore, and has a little knife and fork and silver mug at home, so girlish is she): I say, in a word—and I believe without fear of contradiction—that I delighted everybody.

"Delightful man!" said MRS. BANGLES to my excellent friend, MRS. GOLDMORE.

"Extraordinary creature; so odd, isn't he?" replied that admirable woman.

"What a flow of spirits he has!" cried the charming VIOLET.

"And yet sorrows repose under that smiling mask, and those outbreaks of laughter perhaps conceal the groans of smouldering passion and the shrieks of withering despair," sighed FLORENCE. "It is always so; the wretched *seem* to be most joyous. If I didn't think that man miserable, I couldn't be happy," she added, and lapsed into silence. Little MRS. DIGGS told me every word of the conversation, when I came up the first of the gentlemen to tea.

"Clever fellow that," said (as I am given to understand) SIR HARCOURT GULPH. "I liked that notion of his about *Croquignoles à la pouffarde:* I will speak to MOUFFLON to try it."

"I really shall mention in the Bank parlour to-morrow," the Director remarked, "what he said about the present crisis, and his project for a cast-iron currency: that man is by no means the trifler he pretends to be."

"Where did he serve?" asked BANGLES. "If he can manœuvre an army as well as he talks about it, demmy, he ought to be Commander-in-Chief. Did you hear, CAPTAIN DE BOSKY, what he said about pontooning the echelons, and operating with our reserve upon the right bank of the river at Ferozeshah?' Gad, Sir, if that manœuvre had been performed, not a man of the Sikh army would have escaped:"—in which case of course MAJOR BANGLES would have lost the black tiger behind his cab; but DE BOSKY did not make this remark. The great stupid hulking wretch remarked nothing; he gorged himself with meat and wine, and when quite replete with claret, strutted up to the drawing-room to show his chest and his white waistcoat there.

I was pouring into VIOLET'S ear (to the discomfiture of FLORENCE, who was knocking about the tea-things madly) some of those delightful nothings with which a well-bred man in society entertains a female. I spoke to her about the last balls in London—about FANNY FINCH'S elopement with TOM PARROT, who had nothing but his place in the Foreign Office—about the people who were at Brighton—about MR. MIDGE'S delightful sermon at church last Sunday—about the last fashions, and the next—*que sais-je?*—when that brute DE BOSKY swaggered up.

"Ah, hum, haw," said he, "were you out *raiding* to-day, MISS GOLDMAW?"

Determined to crush this odious and impertinent blunderer, who had no more wit than the horses he bestrides, I resolved to meet him on his own ground, and to beat him even on the subject of horses.

I am sorry to say, my dear PUGSBY, I did not confine myself strictly to truth; but I described how I had passed three months in the Desert with an Arab tribe: how I had a mare during that period, descended fromBoorawk, the mare of the Prophet, which I afterwards sold for 50,000 piastres to MAHOMET ALI; and how, being at Trebizond, smoking with the sanguinary Pasha of that place, I had bitted, saddled, and broke to carry a lady, a grey Turkoman horse of his, which had killed fourteen of his grooms, and bit off the nose of his Kislar Aga.

"Do join us in our ride to-morrow," cried VIOLET; "the downs are delightful."

"Fairest lady, to hear is to obey," answered I, with a triumphant glance at DE BOSKY. I had done *his* business, at any rate.

Well, Sir, I came at two o'clock, mounted on one of JIGGOT's hacks—an animal that I know, and that goes as easy as a sedan-chair, and found the party assembling before the Director's house, in the King's Parade. There was young GOLDMORE—the lovely VIOLET, in a habit that showed her form to admiration, and a perfectly ravishing Spanish tuft in her riding-hat, with a little gold whip and a little pair of gauntlets—*à croquer*, in a word. MAJOR BANGLES and lady were also of the party; in fact we were 'a gallant company of cavaliers,' as JAMES says in his novels; and with my heels well down, and one of my elbows stuck out, I looked, Sir, like the MARQUIS OF ANGLESEA. I had the honour of holding VIOLET's little foot in my hand, as she jumped into her saddle. She sprang into it like a fairy.

Last of all the stupid DE BOSKY came up. He came up moaning and groaning. "I have had a kick in the back from a horse in the livery-stables," says he; "I can't hold this horse; will you ride him,

CANTERBURY?" His horse was a black, wicked-looking beast as ever I saw, with blood-shot eyes and a demoniacal expression.

What could I do, after the stories about Boorawk and the PASHA OF TREBIZOND? Sir, I was obliged to get off my sedan-chair and mount the Captain's Purgatory, as I call him—a disgusting brute, and worthy of his master.

Well, Sir, off we set—Purgatory jumping from this side of the road to t'other, shying at MISS POGSON, who passed in her carriage (as well he might at so hideous a phenomenon)—plunging at an apple-woman and stall—going so wild at a baker's cart that I thought he would have jumped into the hall-door where the man was delivering a pie for dinner—and flinging his head backwards so as to endanger my own nose every moment. It was all I could do to keep him in. I tugged at both bridles till I tore his jaws into a fury, I suppose.

Just as we were passing under the viaduct, whirr came the streaming train with a bang, and a shriek, and a whizz. The brute would hold in no longer: he ran away with me.

I stuck my feet tight down in the stirups, and thought of my mother with inexpressible agony. I clutched hold of all the reins and a great deal of the mane of the brute. I saw trees, milestones, houses, villages, pass away from me—away, away, away—

away—by the corn-fields—away by the wolds—away by the eternal hills—away by the woods and precipices—the woods, the rocks, the villages flashed by me. O, PUGSBY! how I longed for the Megatherium during that ride!

It lasted, as it seemed to me, about nine hours, during which I went over, as I should think, about 540 miles of ground. I didn't come off—my hat did, a new Lincoln and Bennett, but I didn't—and at length the infuriate brute paused in his mad career, with an instinctive respect for the law, at a turnpike gate. I little knew the blessing of a turnpike until then.

In a minute BANGLES came up, bursting with laughter. "You can't manage that horse, I think, said the Major, with his infernal good nature. "Shall I ride him? Mine is a quiet beast."

I was off Purgatory's back in a minute, and as I mounted on BANGLES' hackney, felt as if I was getting into bed, so easy, so soft, so downy he seemed to me.

He said, though I never can believe it, that we had only come about a mile and a half; and at this moment the two ladies and DE BOSKY rode up.

"Is that the way you broke the PASHA OF TREBIZOND's horse?" VIOLET said. I gave a laugh; but it was one of despair. I should have liked to plunge a dagger in DE BOSKY's side.

I shall come to town directly, I think. This Brighton is a miserable Cockney place.

TRAVELLING NOTES

BY OUR FAT CONTRIBUTOR.

[The relations, friends, and creditors of the singular and erratic being who, under the title of the Fat Contributor (he is, by the way, the thinnest mortal that ever was seen), wrote some letters in August last in this periodical, have been alarmed by the sudden cessation of his correspondence; and the public, as we have reason to know from the innumerable letters we have received, has participated in this anxiety.

Yesterday by the Peninsular and Oriental Company's steam-ship Tagus, we received a packet of letters in the strange handwriting of our eccentric friend; they are without date, as might be expected from the author's usual irregularity, but the first three letters appear to have been written at sea, between Southampton and Gibraltar, the last from the latter-named place. The letters contain some novel descriptions of the countries which our friend visited, some neat and apposite moral sentiments, and some animated descriptions of maritime life; we therefore hasten to lay them before the public.

He requests us to pay his laundress in Lincoln's Inn, "a small forgotten account." As we have not the honour of that lady's acquaintance, and as no doubt she reads this Miscellany (in company with every lady of the land), we beg her to apply at our Office, where her claim, upon authentication, shall be settled].

Having been at Brussels for three whole days (during which time I calculate, I ate no less than fifty-four dishes at that admirable *table-d'hôte* at the Hôtel de Suède); time began to hang heavily upon me. Although I am fat, I am one of the most active men in the Universe—in fact, I roll like a ball—and possess a love of locomotion which would do credit to the leanest of travellers, George Borrow, Captain Clapperton, or Mungo Park. I therefore pursued a rapid course to Paris, and thence to Havre.

As Havre is the dullest place on earth, I quitted it the next day by the *Ariadne* steamer—the weather was balm, real balm. A myriad of twinkling stars glittered down on the deck which bore the Fat Contributor to his native shores—the crescent moon shone in a sky of the most elegant azure, and myriads of dimples decked the smiling countenance of the peaceful main. I was so excited I would not turn into bed, but paced the quarter-deck all night, singing my favourite sea songs— all the pieces out of all the operas which I had ever heard, and many more tunes which I invented on the spot, but have forgotten long since.

I never passed a more delicious night. I lay down happily to rest, folded in my cloak—the eternal stars above me, and beneath me a horse-hair mattress, which the steward brought from below. When I rose like a giant refreshed at morn, Wight was passed; the two churches of Southampton lay on my right hand; we were close to the pier.

"What is yonder steamer?" I asked of the steward, pointing to a handsome, slim, black craft that lay in the harbour, a flag of blue, red, white, and yellow, on one mast; a blue peter (signal of departure) at another.

"That," said the steward, "is the Peninsular and Oriental Steam Navigation Company's ship, *Lady Mary Wood.* She leaves port to-day for Gibraltar, touching on her way at Vigo, Oporto, Lisbon and Cadiz."

I quitted the *Ariadne*—Jason did the same in Lemprière's Dictionary, and she consoled herself with drinking, it is said—I quitted the ship, and went to the inn, with the most tremendous thoughts heaving, panting, boiling, in my bosom!

"Lisbon!" I said, as I cut into a cold round of beef for breakfast, (if I have been in foreign parts for a week, I always take cold beef and ale for breakfast,) "Lisbon!" I exclaimed, "the fleuve der Tage! the orange groves of Cintra! the vast towers of Mafra Belem, the Gallegos, and the Palace of Necessidades! Can I see all these in a week? Have I courage enough to go and see them?" I took another cut at the beef.

"What!" continued I (my mouth full of muffin), "is it possible that I, sitting here as I am, may without the least trouble, and at a trifling expense, transport myself to Cadiz, shining o'er the dark blue sea, to the land of the Sombrero and the Seguidilla—of the puchera, the muchacha, and the Abanico? If I employ my time well, I may see a bull-fight, an *auto-da-fé*, or at least a revolution. I may look at the dark eyes of the Andalusian maid flashing under the dark meshes of her veil; and listen to ALMAVIVA's guitar, as it tinkles under the balcony of ROSINA?—What time does the *Mary Wood* go, waiter?" I cried.

The slave replied she went at half-past three.

"And does she make Gibraltar?" I continued. "Say, JOHN, will she land me at Gibel el Altar? opposite the coasts of Afric, whence whilom swarmed the galleys of the Moor, and landed on the European shores the dusky squadrons of the Moslemah? Do you mean to say, THOMAS, that if I took my passage in yon boat, a few days would transport me to the scene renowned in British story—the fortress seized by ROOK, and guarded by ELLIOT? Shall I be able to see the smoking ruins of Tangiers, which the savage bully of Gaul burned down in braggadocio pride?"

"Would you like anything for dinner before you go?" WILLIAM here rather sulkily interrupted me, "I can't be a listening to you all day—there's the bell of 24 ringing like mad."

My repast was by this time concluded—the last slice of boiled beef made up my mind completely. I went forth to the busy town—I sought a ready-made linen warehouse—and in the twinkling of an eye I purchased all that was necessary for a two months' voyage.

From that moment I let my mustachios grow. At a quarter-past three, a mariner of a stout but weather-beaten appearance, with a quantity of new carpet-bags and portmanteaus, containing twenty-four new shirts (six terrifically striped), two dozen ditto stockings—in brief, everything necessary for travel, tripped lightly up the ladder of the *Lady Mary Wood.*

I made a bow as I have seen T. P. Cooke do it on the stage. "Avast there, my hearty," I said, "can you tell me which is the skipper of this here craft, and can a seaman get a stowage in her?"

"I am the captain," said the gentleman, rather surprised.

"Tip us your daddle, then, my old sea-dog, and give us change for this here Henry Hase."

'Twas a bank note for 100*l.* and the number was 33769.

II.

THE SHIP AT SEA.—DOLORES!

The first thing that a narrow-minded individual does on shipboard is to make his own berth comfortable at the expense of his neighbours. The next is to criticise the passengers round about him.

Do you remark, when Britons meet, with what a scowl they salute each other, as much as to say, "Bless your eyes, what the angel do you do here?" *Young* travellers, that is to say, adopt this fascinating mode of introduction—I am old in voyaging—I go up with a bland smile to one and every passenger. I originate some clever observation about the fineness of the weather—if there are ladies, I manage to make some side appeal to *them*, which is sure of a tender appreciation: above all, if there are old ladies, fat ladies, very dropsical, very sea-sick, or ugly ladies, I pay them some delicate attention—I go up and insinuate a pillow under their poor feet. In the intervals of sickness I whisper, "a leetle hot sherry and water!" All these little kindnesses act upon their delicate hearts, and I know that they say to themselves, "How exceedingly polite and well-bred that stout young man is."

"It's a pity he's so fat," says one.

"Yes, but then he's so active," ejaculates another.

And thus you, my dear and ingenuous youth who read this, and whom I recommend to lay to heart every single word of it—I am adored by all my fellow passengers. When they go ashore they feel a pang at parting with their amiable companion. I am only surprised that I have not been voted several pieces of plate upon these occasions—perhaps, dear youth, if you follow my example you may be more lucky.

Acting upon this benevolent plan, I shall not begin satirically to describe the social passengers that tread with me the deck of the *Lady Mary Wood.*

I shall not, like that haughty and supercilious wretch with the yellow whiskers, yonder, cut short the gentle efforts at good fellowship which human beings around me may make—or grumble at the dinner, or the head-wind, or the narrowness of the berths, or the jarring of the engines—but shall make light of all these—nay, by ingenuity, turn them to a facetious and moral purpose. Here, for instance, is a picture of the ship, taken under circumstances of great difficulty—over the engine-room—the funnel snorting, the ship's sides throbbing, as if in a fit of ague.

There! I flatter myself that is a master-piece of perspective. If the Royal Academy would exhibit, or Mr. Moon would publish a large five guinea plate of the "main-deck of a steamer," how the public would admire and purchase! With a little imagination, you may fancy yourself on shipboard. Before you is the iron grating, up to which you see peeping every minute the pumping head of the engine; on the right is the galley, where the cook prepares the victuals that we eat or not, as weather permits, near which stands a living likeness of Mr. Jones, the third engineer; to the left and running along the side of the paddle-boxes are all sorts of mysterious little houses painted green, from which mates, mops, cabin-boys, black engineers, and oily cook's-assistants emerge; above is the deck between the two paddle-boxes on which the captain walks in his white trousers and telescope (you may catch a glimpse of the former), and from which in bad weather he, speaking-trumpet in hand, rides the whirlwind and directs the storm. Those are the buckets in case of fire; see how they are dancing about! because they have nothing else to do—I trust they will always remain idle. A ship on fire is a conveyance by which I have no mind to travel.

Farther away, by the quarter-deck ladder, you see accurate portraits of MESSRS. MAC WHIRTER and MAC MURDO, of Oporto and St. Mary's, wine-merchants; and far, far away, on the quarter-deck, close by the dark helmsman, with the binnacle shining before his steadfast eyes, and the English flag streaming behind him (it is a confounded head-wind) —you see—O my wildly beating, my too susceptible heart!—you see DOLORES!

I write her name with a sort of despair. I think it is four hours ago since I wrote that word on the paper. They were at dinner, but (for a particular reason) I cared not to eat, and sat at my desk apart. The dinner went away, either down the throats of the eager passengers, or to the black caboose whence it came—dessert passed—the sun set—tea came—the moon rose—she is now high in heaven, and the steward is laying the supper things, and all this while I have been thinking of DOLORES, DOLORES, DOLORES!

She is a little far off in the picture; but by the aid of a microscope, my dear sir, you may see every lineament of her delicious countenance—every fold of the drapery which adorns her fair form, and falls down to the loveliest foot in the world! Did you ever see anything like that ankle?—those thin, open-worked stockings make my heart thump in an indescribable rapture. I would drink her health out of that shoe; but I swear it would not hold more than a liqueur glass of wine. Before she left us—ah me! that I should have to write the words *left us*—I tried to make her likeness; but the abominable brute of a steam-engine shook so, that—would you believe it?—this is all I could make of the loveliest face in the world!

I look even at that with a melancholy pleasure. It is not very like her, certainly; but it was drawn from her—it is not the rose, but it has been near it. Her complexion is a sort of gold colour—her eyes of a melting, deep, unfathomably deep brown—and as for her hair, the varnish of my best boots for evening parties is nothing compared to it for blackness and polish.

She used to sit on the quarter-deck of sunny afternoons, and smoke paper cigars—oh if you could have seen how sweetly she smiled and how prettily she puffed out the smoke! I have got a bit of one of them which has been at her sweet lips. I shall get a gold box to keep it in some day when I am in cash. There she sat smoking, and the young rogues of the ship used to come crowding round her. Mac Whirter was sorry she didn't stop at Oporto, Mac Murdo was glad because she was going to Cadiz—I warrant he was—my heart was burst asunder with a twang and a snap, and she carried away half of it in the Malta boat, which bore her away from me for ever. Dolores was not like your common mincing English girls—she had always a repartee and a joke upon her red lips which made every one around her laugh—some of these jokes I would repeat were it not a breach of confidence; and had they not been uttered in the Spanish language, of which I don't understand a word. So I used to sit quite silent and look at her full in the face for hours and hours, and offer her my homage that way.

You should have seen how Dolores ate too! Our table was served four times a-day—at breakfast, with such delicacies as beefsteaks, bubble and squeak, fried ham and eggs, hashed goose, twice-laid, &c.,—of all which trifles little Dolores would have her share—the same at dinner when she was well: and—when beneath the influence of angry Neptune the poor soul was stretched in the berth of sickness, the stewards would nevertheless bear away plates upon plates of victuals to the dear suffering girl; and it would be "Irish stew for a lady, if you please, sir?"—"rabbit and onions for the ladies' cabin"—"Duck, if you please, and plenty of stuffing, for the Spanish lady." And such is our blind partiality when the heart is concerned, that I admired that conduct in my DOLORES which I should have detested in other people. For instance, if I had seen MISS JONES or MISS SMITH making peculiar play with her knife, or pulling out a tooth-pick after dinner, what would have been my feelings?

But I only saw perfection in DOLORES.

III.

FROM MY LOG-BOOK AT SEA.

WE are at sea—yonder is Finisterre.

The only tempest I have to describe during the voyage is that raging in my own stormy interior. It is most provokingly uncomfortably fine weather. As we pass Ushant there is not a cloud on the sky, there scarcely seems a ripple on the water—and yet—oh yet! it is not a calm *within*. Passion and sea-sickness are raging there tumultuously.

Why is it I cannot eat my victuals? Why is it that when Steward brought to my couch a plateful of Sea-Pie (I called wildly for it, having read of the dish in maritime novels), why is it that the onions of which that delectable condiment seems to be mainly composed, caused a convulsive shudder to pass from my nose through my whole agonised frame, obliging me to sink back gasping in the crib, and to forego all food for many, many hours?

I think it must be my love for DOLORES that causes this deperate disinclination for food, and yet I have been in love many times before, and I don't recollect ever having lost my desire for my regular four meals a day. I believe I must be very far gone this time.

I ask FRANK, the Steward, how is the Señora? She suffers, the dear, dear soul! She is in the ladies' cabin—she has just had a plate of roast-pork carried in to her.

She always chooses the dishes with onions—she comes from the sunny South, where both onions and garlic are plentifully used—and yet somehow, in the depression of my spirits—I wish, I wish she hadn't a partiality for that particular vegetable.

It is the next day. I have lost almost all count of time; and only know how to trace it faintly, by remembering the Champagne days—Thursday and Sunday.

I am abominably hungry. And yet when I tried at breakfast!—O horror!—I was obliged to plunge back to the little cabin again, and have not been heard of since. Since then I have been lying on my back, sadly munching biscuit and looking at the glimmer of the sun through the deadlight overhead.

I *was* on the sofa, enjoying (if a wretch so miserable can be said to enjoy anything) the fresh breeze which came through the open port-hole, and played upon my dewy brow. But a confounded great wave came flouncing in at the orifice, blinded me, wet me through, wet all my linen in the carpet-bag, rusted all my razors, made water-buckets of my boots, and played the deuce with a tin of sweet biscuits which have formed my only solace.

"Ha! Ha! What do I want with boots and razors? I could not put on a boot now if you were to give me a thousand guineas. I could not shave if my life depended on it. I think I could cut my head off—but the razors are rusty and would not cut clean. O DOLORES, DOLORES!

The hunger grows worse and worse. It seems to me an age since butcher's meat passed these lips: and, to add to my misery, I can hear every word the callous wretches are saying in the cabin; the clatter of the plates, the popping of the soda-water corks—or, can it be Champagne day, and I a miserable groveller on my mattress? The following is the conversation:—

Captain. MR. JONES, may I have honour of a

glass of wine? FRANK, some Champagne to MR. JONES.

Colonel Condy (of the Spanish service). That's a mighty delicate ham, Mr. Carver, may I thrubble ye for another slice?

Mr. Mac Murdo (of St. Mary's, sherry-merchant). Where does the Providore get this sherry? If he would send to my cellars in St. Mary's, I would put him in a couple of butts of wine that shouldn't cost him half the money he pays for this.

Mr. Mac Whirter (of Oporto). The sherry's good enough for sherry, which is never worth the drinking; but the port is abominable. Why doesn't he come to our house for it?

Captain. There is nothing like leather, gentlemen.—More Champagne, FRANK—MR. BUNG, try the maccaroni. MR. PERKINS, this plum-pudding is capital.

Steward. Some pudding for MRS. BIGBODY in the cabin, and another slice of duck for the Señora.

And so goes on the horrid talk. They are eating —*she* is eating; they laugh, they jest. MR. SMITH jocularly enquires, How is the fat gentleman that was so gay on board the first day? Meaning *me*, of course; and I am lying supine in my berth, without even strength enough to pull the rascal's nose. I detest SMITH.

Friday.—Vigo; its bay; beauty of its environs. —Nelson.

Things look more briskly; the swell has gone down. We are upon deck again. We have breakfasted. We have made up for the time lost in abstinence during the two former days. DOLORES is on deck; and when the spring sun is out, where should the butterfly be but on the wing? DOLORES is the sun, I am the remainder of the simile.

It is astonishing how a few hours' calm can make one forget the long hours of weary bad weather. I can't fancy I have been ill at all, but for those melancholy observations scrawled feebly down in pencil in my journal yesterday. I am in clean shining white-ducks, my blue shirt-collars falling elegantly over a yellow bandanna. My moustachios have come on wonderfully; they are a little red or so. But the Spanish, they say, like fair faces. I would do any thing for DOLORES but smoke with her; *that* I confess I dare not attempt.

It appears it was THE BAY OF BISCAY that made me so ill. We were in Vigo yesterday (a plague take it! I have missed what is said to be one of the most beautiful bays in the world); but I was ill, and getting a little sleep; and when it is known as a fact that a NELSON was always ill on first going to sea, need a Fat Contributor be ashamed of a manly and natural weakness?

Saturday.—Description of Oporto.

We were off the bar at an exceedingly early hour—so early, that although a gun fired and waked me out of a sound sleep, I did not rise to examine the town.

It is three miles inland, and therefore cannot be seen. It is famous for the generous wine which bears the name of port, and is drunk by some after dinner; by other, and I think wiser persons, simply after cheese.

As about ten times as much of this liquor is drunk in England as is made in Portugal, it is needless to institute any statistical inquiries into the growth and consumption of the wine.

Oporto was besieged by Don Miguel, the rightful king, who, although he had Marshal Bourmont and justice on his side, was defeated by Don Pedro and British Valour. Thus may our arms ever triumph! These are the only facts I was enabled to gather regarding Oporto.

New Passengers.—On coming on deck, I was made aware that we had touched land by the presence on the boat of at least a hundred passengers, who had not before appeared among us. They had come from Vigo, and it appears were no more disposed to rouse at the morning gun than I was.

They were Gallegos going to Lisbon for service;

and I wished that a better hand than mine—viz., one of those immortal pencils which decorate the columns of our dear *Punch*—had been there to take cognizance of these strange children of the South—in their scarfs and their tufted hats, with their brown faces shining as they lay under the sun.

Nor were these the only new passengers; with them came on board a half-dozen of Hungarian cloth-sellers, one of whom as he lay upon two barrels, slept the sleep of innocence *sub Jove.*

Again the same individual, but ah how changed! He is suffering from the pangs of sea-sickness, and I have no doubt yearning for fatherland, or land of some sort. But I am interrupted. Hark! 'tis the bell for lunch! *

* Though our fat friend's log has been in the present instance a little tedious, the observant reader may nevertheless draw from it a complete and agreeable notion of the rise, progress, and conclusion of the malady of sea-sickness. He is exhausted; he is melancholy; he is desperate; he rejects his victuals; he grows hungry, but dares not eat; he mends; his spirits rise; all his faculties are restored to him; and he eats with redoubled vigour. This fine diagnosis of the maritime complaint, we pronounce from experience may be perfectly relied upon.

PUNCH IN THE EAST.

FROM OUR FAT CONTRIBUTOR.

I.

On board the P. & O. Company's Ship,
"Burrumpooter," off Alexandria.

FAT CONTRIBUTOR, indeed! I lay down my pen, and smiling in bitter scorn as I write the sarcastic title—I remember it was that which I assumed when my peregrinations began. It is now an absurd misnomer.

I forget whence I wrote to you last. We were but three weeks from England, I think—off Cadiz, or Malta, perhaps—I was full of my recollections of Dolores—full in other ways, too. I have travelled in the East since then. I have seen the gardens of Bujukdere and the kiosks of the Seraglio: I have seen the sun sinking behind Morea's hills, and rising over the red waves of the Nile. I have travelled like BENJAMIN D'ISRAELI, ULYSSES, MONCKTON MILNES, and the eminent sages of all times. I am not the fat being I was, (and proudly styled myself,) when I left my dear, dear Pall Mall. You recollect my Nugee dress-coat, with the brass buttons and Canary silk lining, that the Author of the "Spirit of the Age" used to envy? I never confessed it—but I was in agonies when I wore that coat. I was girthed in (inwardly) so tight, that I thought every day after the third *entrée* apoplexy would ensue—and had my name and address written most legibly in the breast flap, so that I might be carried home in case I was found speechless in the street on my return from dinner. A smiling face often hides an aching heart; I promise you mine did in that coat, and not my heart only, but other regions. There is a skeleton in every house—and mine—no—I wasn't exactly a skeleton in that garment, but suffered secret torments in it, to which, as I take it, those of the Inquisition were trifles.

I put it on t'other day to dine with BUCKSHEESH PASHA at Grand Cairo—I could have buttoned the breast over to the two buttons behind. My dear Sir—I looked like a perfect GUY. I am wasted away—a fading flower—I don't weigh above sixteen and a half now. Eastern Travel has done it—and all my fat friends may read this and consider it. It is something at least to know. BYRON (one of *us*) took vinegar and starved himself to get down the disagreeable plenitude. Vinegar?—nonsense!—try Eastern travel. I am bound to say, however, that it don't answer in all cases. WADDILOVE, for instance, with whom I have been making the journey, has bulged out in the sun like a pumpkin, and at dinner you see his coat and waistcoat buttons spirt violently off his garments—no longer able to bear the confinement there. One of them hit COLONEL SOURCILLON plump on the nose, on which the Frenchman * * But to return to my own case. A man always speaks most naturally and truly of that which occurs to himself.

I attribute the diminution in my size not to my want of appetite, which has been uniformly good. Pale ale is to be found universally throughout Turkey, Syria, Greece, and Egypt, and after a couple of foaming bottles of Bass, a man could eat a crocodile (we had some at BUCKSHEESH PASHA'S, fattened in the tanks of his country villa of El Muddee, on the Nile, but tough—very fishy and tough)—the appetite, I say, I have found to be generally good in these regions—and attribute the corporeal diminution solely TO WANT OF SLEEP.

I give you my word of honour, as a gentleman, *that for seven weeks I have never slept a single wink.* It is my belief that nobody does in the East. You get to do without it perfectly. It may be said of these countries, they are so hospitable, you are never alone. You have always friends to come and pass the night with you, and keep you alive with their cheerful innocent gambols. At Constantinople, at Athens, Malta, Cairo, Gibraltar, it is all the same. Your watchful friends persist in paying you attention. The frisky and agile flea, the slow but steady-purposed bug—the fairy mosquito, with his mellow-sounding-horn, rush to welcome the stranger to their shores—and never leave him during his stay. At first, and before you are used to the manners of the country, the attention is rather annoying.

Man is a creature of habit. I did not at first like giving up my sleep. I had been used to it in England. I occasionally repined as my friends persisted in calling my attention to them, grew sulky and peevish, wished myself in bed in London—nay, in the worst bed in the most frequented old, mouldy, musty, wooden-galleried coach inn in Aldgate or Holborn. I recollect a night at the Bull, in poor dear old MRS. NELSON's time—well, well, it is nothing to the East. What a country would this be for TIFFIN, and what a noble field for his labours!

Though I am used to it now, I can't say but it is probable that when I get back to England I shall return to my old habits. Here, on board the Peninsular and Oriental Company's magnificent steamship, *Burrumpooter*, I thought of trying whether I could sleep any more. I had got the sweetest little cabin in the world; the berths rather small and tight for a man of still considerable proportions—but everything as neat, sweet, fresh and elegant as the most fastidious amateur of the night-cap might desire. I hugged the idea of having the little palace all to myself. I placed a neat white night-gown and my favourite pink silk cap, on the top berth ready. The sea was as clear as glass—the breeze came cool and refreshing through the port-hole—the towers of Alexandria faded away as our ship sailed westward. My Egyptian friends were left behind. It would soon be sunset. I longed for that calm hour, and meanwhile went to enjoy myself at dinner with a hundred and forty passengers from Suez, who laughed and joked, drank Champagne and the exhilarating Hodgson, and brought the latest news from Dumdum Futtyghur.

I happened to sit next at table to the French gentleman before mentioned, Colonel Sourcillon, in the service of the Rajah of Lahore, returning to Europe on leave of absence. The Colonel is six feet high—of a grim and yellow physiognomy, with a red ribbon at his button-hole, of course, and large black mustachios, curling up to his eyes—to one eye, that is—the other was put out in mortal combat, which has likewise left a furious purple gash down one cheek, a respectable but terrible sight.

"Vous regardez ma cicatrice," said the Colonel, perceiving that I eyed him with interest. "Je l'ai reçue en Espagne, Monsieur, à la bataille de Vittoria, que nous avons gagnée sur vous. J'ai tué de ma main le grrredin de Feldmaréchal Anglais qui m'a donné cette noble blessure. Elle n'est pas la seule, Monsieur. Je possède encore soixante-quatorze cicatricees sur le corps. Mais j'ai fait sonner partout le grrrand nom de la Frrance. Vous êtes militaire, Monsieur? Non? Passez moi le poivre-rouge, s'il vous plait."

The Colonel emptied the cayenne pepper cruet over his fish, and directed his conversation entirely to me. He told me that ours was a perfidious nation, that he esteemed some individuals, but detested the country, which he hoped to see *écrrasé un jour*. He said I spoke French with remarkable purity; that on board all our steamers there was an infamous conspiracy to insult every person bearing the name of Frenchman; that he would call out the Captain directly they came ashore; that he could not even get a cabin; had I one? On my affirmative reply, he said I was a person of such amiable manners, and so unlike my countrymen, that he would share my cabin with me—and instantly shouted to the steward to put his trunks into number 202.

What could I do? When I went on deck to smoke a cigar, the Colonel retired, pretending a *petite santé*, suffering a horrible *mal de mer*, and dreadful shooting pains in thirty-seven of his wounds. What, I say, could I do? I had not the cabin to myself. He had a right to sleep there—at any rate, I had the best berth, and if he did not snore, my rest would not be disturbed.

But ah! my dear friends—when I thought I would go down and sleep—the first sleep after seven weeks—fancy what I saw—he was asleep in my berth.

His sword, gun, and pistol-cases, blocked up the other sleeping-place; his bags, trunks, pipes, cloaks, and portmanteaus, every corner of the little room.

"QUI VA LA?" roared the monster, with a terrific oath, as I entered the cabin. "Ah! c'est vous, Monsieur, pourquoi diable faîtes-vous tant de bruit? J'ai une petite santé; laissez moi dormir en paix."

I went upon deck. I shan't sleep till I get back to England again. I paid my passage all the way home: but I stopped, and am in quarantine at Malta. I couldn't make the voyage with that Frenchman. I have no money; send me some, and relieve the miseries of him who was once

THE FAT CONTRIBUTOR.

II.

ON THE PROSPECTS OF PUNCH IN THE EAST.

To the Editor of Punch (Confidential).

MY DEAR SIR—In my last letter (which was intended for the public eye), I was too much affected by the recollection of what I may be permitted to call the ARABIAN NIGHTS' ENTERTAINMENTS, to allow me for the moment to commit to paper that useful information, in the imparting of which your Journal—*our* Journal—the world's Journal—yields to none, and which the British public will naturally expect from all who contribute to your columns. I address myself therefore privately to you, so that you may deal with the facts I may communicate as you shall think best for the general welfare.

What I wish to point out especially to your notice is, the astonishing progress of *Punch* in the East. Moving according to your orders in strict incognito, it has been a source of wonder and delight to me to hear how often the name of the noble Miscellany was in the mouths of British men. At Gibraltar its jokes passed among the midshipmen, merchants, Jews, &c., assembled at the hotel table (and quite unconscious how sweetly their words sounded on the ear of a silent guest at the board) as current, ay, much more current, than the coin of the realm. At Malta, the first greeting between CAPTAIN TAGUS and some other Captain in anchor-buttons, who came to hail him when we entered harbour, related to *Punch*. "What's the news?" exclaimed the other Captain. "Here's *Punch*," was the immediate reply of TAGUS, handing it out—and the other Captain's face was suffused with instant smiles as his enraptured eye glanced over some of the beauteous designs of LEECH. At Athens, MR. SMITH, second-cousin of the respected Vice-Consul, who came to our inn, said to me mysteriously, "I'm told we've got *Punch* on board." I took him aside, and pointed him out (in confidence) MR. WADDILOVE, the stupidest man of all our party, as the author in question.

Somewhat to my annoyance (for I was compelled to maintain my privacy), MR. W. was asked to a splendid dinner in consequence — a dinner which ought by rights to have fallen to my share. It was a consolation to me however to think, as I ate my solitary repast at one of the dearest and worst inns I ever entered, that though *I* might be overlooked, *Punch* was respected in the land of SOCRATES and PERICLES.

At the Piræus we took on board four young gentlemen from Oxford, who had been visiting the scenes consecrated to them by the delightful associations of the Little Go; and as they paced the deck and looked at the lambent stars that twinkled on the bay once thronged with the galleys of THEMISTOCLES,— what, sir, do you think was the song they chanted in chorus? Was it a lay of burning SAPPHO? Was it a thrilling ode of ALCÆUS? No; it was—

> "Had I an ass averse to speed,
> Deem ye I'd strike him? no, indeed," &c.

which you had immortalised, I recollect, in your Vol. 6! (Donkeys, it must be premised, are most numerous and flourishing in Attica, commonly bestridden by the modern Greeks, and no doubt extensively popular among the ancients—unless human nature has very much changed since their time.) Thus we find that *Punch* is respected at Oxford as well as in Athens, and I trust at Cambridge, likewise.

As we sailed through the blue Bosphorus at midnight, the Health of *Punch* was enthusiastically drunk in the delicious beverage which shares his respectable name; and the ghosts of HERO and LEANDER must have been startled at hearing songs appropriate to the toast, and very different from those with which I have no doubt they amused each other in times so affectingly described in LEMPRIERE's delightful Dictionary. I did not see the Golden Horn at Constantinople, nor hear it blown, probably on account of the fog; but this I can declare, that *Punch* was on the table at Miestre's Hotel, Pera, the spirited proprietor of which little knew that one of its humblest contributors ate his pilaff. Pilaff, by the way, is very good: kabobs are also excellent; my friend, MECHMET EFFENDI, who keeps the kabob shop, close by the Rope-bazaar in Constantinople, sells as good as any in town. At the Armenian shops, too, you get a sort of raisin wine at two piastres a bottle, over which a man can spend an agreeable half hour. I did not hear what the SULTAN ABDUL MEDJID thinks of *Punch*, but of wine he is said to be uncommonly fond.

At Alexandria, there lay the picture of the dear and venerable old face, on the table of the British hotel; and the 140 passengers from Burrumtollah, Chowringhee, &c. (now on their way to England per *Burrumpooter*), rushed upon it—it was the July number, with my paper, which you may remember made such a sensation—even more eagerly than on pale ale. I made cautious inquiries amongst them (never breaking the incognito) regarding the influence of *Punch* in our vast Indian territories. They say that from Cape Comorin to the Sutlege, and from the Sutlege to the borders of Thibet, nothing is talked of but *Punch*. DOST MAHOMMED never misses a single number; and the Tharawaddie knows the figure of LORD BROUGHAM and his Scotch trowsers, as well as that of his favourite vizier. *Punch*, my informant states, has rendered his Lordship so popular throughout our Eastern possessions, that were he to be sent out to India as Governor, the whole army and people would shout with joyful recognition. I throw out this for the consideration of Government at home.

I asked BUCKSHEESH PASHA (with whom I had the honour of dining at Cairo) what his august

Master thought of *Punch*. And AT THE PYRAMIDS—but of these in another letter. You have here enough to show you how kingly the diadem, boundless the sway, of *Punch* is in the East. By it we are enabled to counterbalance the influence of the French in Egypt; by it we are enabled to spread civilisation over the vast Indian Continent, to soothe the irritated feelings of the Sikhs, and keep the Burmese in good humour. By means of *Punch*, it has been our privilege to expose the designs of Russia more effectually than URQUHART ever did, and to this SIR STRATFORD CANNING can testify. A proud and noble post is that which you, Sir, hold over the Intellect of the World; a tremendous power you exercise! May you ever wield it wisely and gently as now! "Subjectis parcere superbos debellare," be your motto! I forget whether I mentioned in my last that I was without funds in quarantine at Fort Manuel, Malta, and shall anxiously expect the favour of a communication from you—*Poste Restante*—at that town.

With assurances of the highest consideration,

Believe me to be, Sir,

Your most faithful Servant and Correspondent,

The F— CONTRIBUTOR.

P. S.—We touched at Smyrna, where I purchased a *real Smyrna sponge*, which trifle I hope your lady will accept for her toilet; some *real Turkey rhubarb* for your dear children; and a friend going to Syria has promised to procure for me *some real Jerusalem artichokes*, which I hope to see flourishing in your garden at ——.

[This letter was addressed "strictly private and confidential" to us: but at a moment when all men's minds are turned towards the East, and every information regarding "the cradle of civilisation" is anxiously looked for, we have deemed it our duty to submit our Correspondent's letter to *the public*. The news which it contains are so important and startling —our correspondent's views of Eastern affairs so novel and remarkable—that they *must* make an impression in Europe. We beg the *Observer*, the *Times*, &c., to have the goodness to acknowledge their authority, if they avail themselves of our facts. And for *us*, it cannot but be a matter of pride and gratification to think—on the testimony of a correspondent who has never deceived us yet—that our efforts for the good of mankind are appreciated by such vast and various portions of the human race, and that our sphere of usefulness is so prodigiously on the increase. Were it not that dinner has been announced (and consequently is getting cold), we would add more. For the present, let us content ourselves by stating that the intelligence conveyed to us is most welcome as it is most surprising, the occasion of heartfelt joy, and, we hope, of deep future meditation.]

III.

ATHENS.

I SEND a picture of some beautiful windmills near Athens, not I believe depicted by any other artist, and which I daresay some people will admire because they are Athenian windmills. The world is made so.

I was not a brilliant boy at school—the only prize I ever remember to have got was in a kind of lottery in which I was obliged to subscribe with seventeen other competitors—and of which the prize was a flogging. That I won. But I don't think I carried off any other. Possibly from laziness, or if you please from incapacity, but I certainly was rather inclined to be of the side of the dunces—SIR WALTER SCOTT, it will be recollected, was of the same species. Many young plants sprouted up round about both of us, I daresay, with astonishing rapidity—but they have gone to seed ere this, or were never worth the cultivation. Great genius is of slower growth.

I always had my doubts about the classics. When I saw a brute of a schoolmaster, whose mind was as coarse-grained as any ploughboy's in Christendom; whose manners were those of the most insufferable of

Heaven's creatures, the English snob trying to turn gentleman; whose lips, when they were not mouthing Greek or grammar, were yelling out the most brutal abuse of poor little cowering gentlemen standing before him: when I saw this kind of man (and the instructors of youth are selected very frequently indeed out of this favoured class) and heard him roar out praises, and pump himself up into enthusiasm for, certain Greek poetry,—I say I had my doubts about the genuineness of the article. A man may well thump you or call you names because you won't learn —but I never could take to the proffered delicacy; the fingers that offered it were so dirty. Fancy the brutality of a man who began a Greek grammar with "τυπτω, I thrash!" We were all made to begin it in that way.

When then I came to Athens, and saw that it was a humbug, I hailed the fact with a sort of gloomy joy. I stood in the Royal Square and cursed the country which has made thousands of little boys miserable. They have blue stripes on the new Greek flag; I thought bitterly of my own. I wished that my schoolmaster had been in the place, that we might have fought there for the right; and that I might have immolated him as a sacrifice to the manes of little boys flogged into premature Hades, or pining away and sickening under the destiny of that infernal Greek grammar. I have often thought that those little cherubs who are carved on tombstones and are represented as possessing a head and wings only, are designed to console little children—usher and beadle-belaboured—and say "there is no flogging where we are." From their conformation, it is impossible. Woe to the man who has harshly treated one of them!

Of the ancient buildings in this beggarly town it is not my business to speak. Between ourselves it must be acknowledged that there was some merit in the Heathens who constructed them. But of the Temple of Jupiter, of which some columns still remain, I declare with confidence that not one of them is taller than our own glorious Monument on Fish-Street-Hill, which I heartily wish to see again, whereas upon the columns of Jupiter I never more desire to set eyes. On the Acropolis and its temples and towers I shall also touch briefly. The frieze of the Parthenon is well-known in England, the famous *chevaux de frieze* being carried off by LORD ELGIN, and now in the British Museum, Great Russell Street, Bloomsbury. The Erectheum is another building, which I suppose has taken its name from the genteel club in London at a corner of St. James's Square. It is likewise called the Temple of Minerva Polias—a capital name for a club in London certainly; fancy gentlemen writing on their cards "MR. JONES, Temple-of-

Minerva-Polias Club."—Our country is surely the most classical of islands.

As for the architecture of that temple, if it be not entirely stolen from St. Prancras Church, New Road, or *vice versâ*, I am a Dutchman. "The Tower of the Winds" may be seen any day at Edinburgh—and the Lantern of Demosthenes is at this very minute perched on the top of the church in Regent Street, within a hundred yards of the lantern of MR. DRUMMOND. Only in London you have them all in much better preservation—the noses of the New Road Caryatides are not broken as those of their sisters here. The temple of the Scotch winds I am pleased to say I have never seen, but I have no doubt it is worthy of the Modern Athens—and as for the Choragic temple of Lysicrates, erroneously called Demosthenes' Lantern—from Waterloo Place you can see it well: whereas here it is a ruin in the midst of a huddle of dirty huts, whence you try in vain to get a good view of it.

When I say of the temple of Theseus (quoting MURRAY's Guide-Book) that "it is a peripteral hexastyle with a pronaos, a posticum and two columns between the antæ," the commonest capacity may perfectly imagine the place. Fancy it upon an irregular ground of copper-coloured herbage, with black goats feeding on it, and the sound of perpetual donkeys braying round about. Fancy to the south-east the purple rocks and towers of the Acropolis meeting the eye—to the south-east the hilly islands and the blue Ægean. Fancy the cobalt sky above, and the temple itself (built of Pentelic marble) of the exact colour and mouldiness of a ripe Stilton cheese, and you have the view before you as well as if you had been there.

As for the modern buildings—there is the Royal Palace, built in the style of High-Dutch-Greek, and resembling Newgate whitewashed and standing on a sort of mangy desert.

The KING'S German guards (Σπιτζβουβοι) have left him perforce; he is now attended by petticoated Albanians, and I saw one of the palace sentries, as the sun was shining on his sentry-box, wisely couched *behind* it.

The Chambers were about to sit when we arrived. The Deputies were thronging to the capital. One of them had come as a third-class passenger of an English steamer, took a first-class place, and threatened to blow out the brains of the steward, who remonstrated with him on the irregularity. It is quite needless to say that he kept his place—and as the honourable deputy could not read, of course he could not be expected to understand the regulations imposed by the avaricious proprietors of the boat in question. Happy is the country to have such makers of laws, and to enjoy the liberty consequent upon the representative system!

Besides OTHO's palace in the great square, there is another house and an hotel; a fountain is going to be erected, and roads even are to be made. At present the KING drives up and down over the mangy plain before-mentioned, and the grand officers of state go up to the palace on donkeys.

As for the Hotel Royal—the Folkstone Hotel might take a lesson from it—they charge five shillings sterling (the coin of the country is the gamma, lambda, and delta, which I never could calculate) for a bed in a double-bedded room; and our poor young friend SCRATCHLEY, with whom I was travelling, was compelled to leave his and sit for safety on a chair, on a table in the middle of the room.

As for me—but I will not relate my own paltry sufferings. The post goes out in half an hour, and I had thought ere its departure to have described to you Constantinople and my interview with the Sultan there—his splendid offers—the PRINCESS BADROULBADOUR, the order of the Nisham, the Pashalic with three tails—and my firm but indignant rejection. I had thought to describe Cairo—interview with MEHEMET ALI—proposals of that Prince—splendid feast at the house of my dear friend BUCKSHEESH PASHA, dancing-girls and magicians after dinner, and their extraordinary disclosures! But I should fill volumes at this rate; and I can't, like MR. JAMES, write a volume between breakfast and luncheon.

I have only time rapidly to jot down my great ADVENTURE AT THE PYRAMIDS—and *Punch's* enthronization there.

IV.

PUNCH AT THE PYRAMIDS.

THE 19th day of October, 1844 (the seventh day of the month Hudjmudj, and the 1229th year of the Mohammedan Hejira, corresponding with the 16,769th anniversary of the 48th incarnation of Veeshnoo), is a day that ought hereafter to be considered eternally famous in the climes of the East and West. I forget what was the day of GENERAL BONAPARTE'S battle of the Pyramids; I think it was in the month Quintidi of the year Nivose of the French Republic, and he told his soldiers that forty centuries looked down upon them from the summit of those buildings—a statement which I very much doubt. But I say THE 19TH DAY OF OCTOBER, 1844, is the most important era in the modern world's history. It unites the modern with the ancient civilisation; it couples the brethren of WATT and COBDEN with the dusky family of PHARAOH and SESOSTRIS; it fuses HERODOTUS with THOMAS BABINGTON MACAULAY; it intertwines the piston of the blond Anglo-Saxon steam-engine with the Needle of the Abyssinian CLEOPATRA; it weds the tunnel of the subaqueous BRUNEL with the mystic edifice of CHEOPS. Strange play of wayward fancy! Ascending the Pyramid, I could not but think of Waterloo Bridge in my dear native London—a building as vast and as magnificent, as beautiful, as useless, and as lonely. Forty centuries have not as yet passed over the latter structure, 'tis true; scarcely an equal number of hackney-coaches have crossed it. But I doubt whether the individuals who contributed to raise it are likely to receive a better dividend for their capital than the swarthy shareholders in the Pyramid speculation, whose dust has long since been trampled over by countless generations of their sons.

If I use in the above sentence the longest words I can find, it is because the occasion is great and demands the finest phrases the dictionary can supply; it is because I have not read TOM MACAULAY in vain; it is because I wish to show I am a dab in history, as the above dates will testify; it is because I have seen the Reverend MR. MILMAN preach in a black gown at Saint Margaret's, whereas at the Coronation he wore a gold cope. The 19th of October was *Punch's Coronation;* I officiated at the august ceremony. To be brief—as illiterate readers may not understand a syllable of the above piece of ornamental eloquence—ON THE 19TH OF OCTOBER, 1844, I PASTED THE GREAT PLACARD OF PUNCH ON THE PYRAMID OF CHEOPS. I did it. The fat contributor did it. If I die, it could not be undone. If I perish, I have not lived in vain.

If the forty centuries *are* on the summit of the Pyramids, as BONAPARTE remarks, all I can say is, *I* did not see them. But *Punch* has really been there; this I swear. One placard I pasted on the first landing-place (who knows how long Arab rapacity will respect the sacred hieroglyphic?). One I placed under a great stone on the summit; one I waved in air, as my Arabs raised a mighty cheer round the peaceful victorious banner; and I flung it towards the sky, which the Pyramid almost touches, and left it to its fate, to mount into the azure vault and take its place among the constellations; to light on the eternal Desert, and mingle with its golden sands; or to flutter and drop into the purple waters of the neighbouring Nile, to swell its fructifying inundations, and mingle with the rich vivifying influence which shoots into the tall palm-trees on its banks, and generates the waving corn.

I wonder were there any signs or omens in London when that event occurred? Did an earthquake take place? Did Stocks or the Barometer preternaturally rise or fall? It matters little. Let it suffice that the thing has been done, and forms an event in History by the side of those other facts to which these prodigious monuments bear testimony. Now to narrate briefly the circumstances of the day.

On Thursday, October 17, I caused my dragoman to purchase in the Frank bazaar at Grand Cairo the following articles, which will be placed in the Museum on my return.

A tin pot, holding about a pint, a packet of flour, and a pig-skin brush of the sort commonly used in Europe—the whole costing about five piastres, or one shilling sterling. They were all the implements needful for this tremendous undertaking.

Horses of the Mosaic Arab breed, I mean those animals called Jerusalem ponies by some in England, by others denominated donkeys, are the common means of transport employed by the subjects of MEHEMET ALI. My excellent friend BUCKSHEESH PASHA would have mounted me either on his favourite horse, or his best dromedary. But I declined those proffers—if I fall, I like better to fall from a short distance than a high one. I have tried tumbling in both ways, and recommend the latter as by far the pleasantest and safest. I chose the Mosaic Arab then—one for the dragoman, one for the requisites of refreshment, and two for myself—not that I proposed to ride two at once, but a person of a certain dimension had best have a couple of animals in case of accident.

I left Cairo on the afternoon of October 18, never hinting to a single person the mighty purpose of my journey. The waters were out, and we had to cross them thrice—twice in track-boats, once on the shoulders of abominable Arabs, who take a pleasure in slipping and in making believe to plunge you in the stream. When in the midst of it, the brutes stop and demand money of you—you are alarmed, the savages may drop you if you do not give—you promise that you will do so. The half-naked ruffians who conduct you up the Pyramid, when they have got you panting to the most steep, dangerous, and lonely stone, make the same demand, pointing downwards while they beg, as if they would fling you in that direction on refusal. As soon as you have breath, you promise more money—it is the best way—you are a fool if you give it when you come down.

The journey I find briefly set down in my pocket-book as thus:—Cairo Gardens—Mosquitoes—Women dressed in blue—Children dressed in nothing—Old Cairo—Nile, dirty water, ferry-boat—Town—Palm-trees, ferry-boat, canal, palm-trees, town—Rice-fields—Maize-fields—Fellows on dromedaries—Donkey down—Over his head—Pick up pieces—More palm-trees—More rice-fields—Water-courses—Howling Arabs—Donkey tumble down again—Inundations—Herons or cranes—Broken bridges—Sands—Pyramids.—If a man cannot make a landscape out of *that* he has no imagination. Let him paint the skies very blue—the sands very yellow—the plains very flat and green—the dromedaries and palm-trees very tall—the women very brown, some with veils, some with nose-rings, some tattooed, and none with stays—and the picture is complete. You may shut your eyes and fancy yourself there. It is the pleasantest way, *entre nous.*

V.

PUNCH AT THE PYRAMIDS.

(Concluded.)

It is all very well to talk of sleeping in the tombs; *that* question has been settled in a former paper, where I have stated my belief that people do not sleep at all in Egypt. I thought to have had some tremendous visions under the shadow of those enormous Pyramids reposing under the stars. Pharaoh or Cleopatra, I thought, might appear to me in a dream. But how could they, as I didn't go to sleep? I hoped for high thoughts, and secret communings with the Spirit of Poesy—I hoped to have let off a sonnet at least, as gentlemen do on visiting the spot—but how could I hunt for rhymes, being occupied all night in hunting for something else? If this remonstrance will deter a single person from going to the Pyramids, my purpose is fully answered.

But *my* case was different. I had a duty to perform—I had to introduce *Punch* to CHEOPS—I had vowed to leave his card at the gates of History—I had a mission, in a word. I roused at sunrise the snoring dragoman from his lair. I summoned the four Arabs who had engaged to assist me in the ascent, and in the undertaking. We lighted a fire of camel's dung at the North-East corner of the Pyramid, just as the god of day rose over Cairo! The embers began to glow, water was put into the tin pot before mentioned,—the pot was put on the fire—'twas a glorious—a thrilling moment!

At 46 minutes past 6, A.M. (by one of DOLLOND'S Chronometers), *the water began to boil.*

At 47 minutes the flour was put gradually into the water—it was stirred with the butt-end of the brush bought for the purpose, and SCHMAKLEK BEG, an Arab, peeping over the pot too curiously, I poked the brush into his mouth at 11 minutes before 7, A.M.

At 7, THE PASTE WAS MADE—doubting whether it was thick enough, SCHMAKLEK tried it with his finger. It was pronounced to be satisfactory.

At 11 minutes past 7, I turned round in a majestic attitude to the four Arabs, and said, "Let us mount." I suggest this scene, this moment, this attitude, to the Committee of the Fine Arts as a proper subject for the Houses of Parliament—*Punch* pointing to the Pyramids, and introducing civilisation to

Egypt—I merely throw it out as a suggestion. What a grand thing the MESSIEURS FOGGO would make of it!

Having given the signal—the Sheikh of the Arabs seized my right arm, and his brother the left. Two volunteer Arabs pushed me (quite unnecessarily) behind. The other two preceded—one with a water-bottle for refreshment; the other with the posters—the pot—the paint-brush and the paste. Away we went—away!

I was blown at the third step. They are exceedingly lofty; about 5 feet high each, I should think—but the ardent spirit will break his heart to win the goal—besides I could not go back if I would. The two Arabs dragged me forward by the arms—the volunteers pushed me up from behind. It was in vain I remonstrated with the latter, kicking violently as occasion offered—they still went on pushing. We arrived at the first landing-place.

I drew out the poster—how it fluttered in the breeze!—with a trembling hand I popped the brush into the paste pot, and smeared the back of the placard, then I pasted up the Standard of our glorious leader—at 19 minutes past 7, by the clock of the great minaret at Cairo, which was clearly visible through my refracting telescope. My heart throbbed when the deed was done. My eyes filled with tears —I am not at liberty to state here all the emotions of triumph and joy which rose in my bosom—so exquisitely overpowering were they. There was *Punch* —familiar old *Punch*—his back to the desert, his beaming face turned towards the Nile.

"Bless him!" I exclaimed, embracing him; and almost choking, gave the signal to the Arabs to move on.

These savage creatures are only too ready to obey an order of this nature. They spin a man along be his size never so considerable. They rattled up to the second landing so swiftly that I thought I should be broken-winded for ever. But they gave us little time to halt. Yallah! Again we mount!—'tis the last and most arduous ascent—the limbs quiver, the pulses beat, the eyes shoot out of the head, the brain reels, the knees tremble and totter, and you are on the summit! I don't know how many hundred thousand feet it is above the level of the sea, but I wonder after that tremendous exercise that I am not a roarer to my dying hour.

When consciousness and lungs regained their play, another copy of the placard was placed under a stone—a third was launched into air in the manner before described, and we gave three immense cheers for *Punch*, which astonished the undiscovered mummies that lie darkling in tomb-chambers, and must have disturbed the broken-nosed old Sphinx who has been couched for thousands of years in the desert hard by. This done, we made our descent from the Pyramids.

And if, my dear Sir, you ask me whether it is worth a man's while to mount up those enormous stones, I will say in confidence that thousands of people went to see the Bottle Conjuror, and that we hear of gentlemen becoming Free-Masons every day.

TRAVELS IN LONDON.

TRAVELS IN LONDON.

THE CURATE'S WALK.

I.

It was the third out of the four bell-buttons at the door at which my friend the curate pulled; and the summons was answered after a brief interval.

I must premise that the house before which we stopped was No. 14, Sedan Buildings, leading out of Great Guelph Street, Dettingen Street, Culloden Street, Minden Square; and Upper and Lower Caroline Row form part of the same quarter—a very queer and solemn quarter to walk in, I think, and one which always suggests Fielding's novels to me. I can fancy Captain Booth strutting out of the very door at which we were standing, in tarnished lace, with his hat cocked over his eye, and his hand on his hanger; or Lady Bellaston's chair and bearers coming swinging down Great Guelph Street, which we have just quitted to enter Sedan Buildings.

Sedan Buildings is a little flagged square, ending

abruptly with the huge walls of BLUCK'S Brewery. The houses, by many degrees smaller than the large decayed tenements in Great Guelph Street, are still not uncomfortable, although shabby. There are brass-plates on the doors, two on some of them; or simple names, as "LUNT," "PADGEMORE," &c. (as if no other statement about LUNT and PADGEMORE were necessary at all) under the bells. There are pictures of mangles before two of the houses, and a gilt arm with a hammer sticking out from one. I never saw a Goldbeater. What sort of a being is he that he always sticks out his ensign in dark, mouldy, lonely, dreary, but somewhat respectable places? What powerful Mulciberian fellows they must be, those Goldbeaters, whacking and thumping with huge mallets at the precious metals all day. I wonder what is Goldbeaters' skin? and do they get impregnated with the metal? and are their great arms under their clean shirts on Sundays, all gilt and shining?

It is a quiet, kind, respectable place somehow, in spite of its shabbiness. Two pewter pints and a jolly little half-pint are hanging on the railings in perfect confidence, basking in what little sun comes into the Court. A group of small children are making an ornament of oyster-shells in one corner. Who has that half-pint? Is it for one of those small ones, or for some delicate female recommended to take beer? The windows in the Court, upon some of which the sun glistens, are not cracked, and pretty clean; it is only the black and dreary look behind which gives them a poverty-stricken appearance. No curtains or blinds. A bird-cage and a very few pots of flowers here and there. This—with the exception of a milkman talking to a whitey-brown woman, made up of bits of flannel and strips of faded chintz and calico seemingly, and holding a long bundle which cried—this was all I saw in Sedan Buildings while we were waiting until the door should open.

At last the door was opened, and by a porteress so small, that I wonder how she ever could have reached up to the latch. She bobbed a curtsey and smiled at the Curate, whose face gleamed with benevolence too, in reply to that salutation.

"Mother not at home?" says FRANK WHITESTOCK, patting the child on the head.

"Mother's out charing, Sir," replied the girl; "but please to walk up, Sir." And she led the way up one and two pair of stairs to that apartment in the house which is called the second floor front; in which was the abode of the charwoman.

There were two young persons in the room, of the respective ages of eight and five, I should think. She of five years of age was hemming a duster, being perched on a chair at the table in the middle of the room. The elder, of eight, politely wiped a chair with a cloth for the accommodation of the good-natured

Curate, and came and stood between his kness, immediately alongside of his umbrella, which also reposed there, and which she by no means equalled in height.

"These children attend my school at St. Timothy's," Mr. Whitestock said; "and Betsy keeps the house whilst her mother is from home."

Anything cleaner or neater than this house it is impossible to conceive. There was a big bed, which must have been the resting-place of the whole of this little family. There were three or four religious prints on the walls; besides two framed and glazed, of Prince Coburg and the Princess Charlotte. There were brass candlesticks, and a lamb on the chimney-piece, and a cupboard in the corner, decorated with near half-a-dozen of plates, yellow bowls, and crockery. And on the table there were two or three bits of dry bread, and a jug with water, with which these three young people (it being then nearly three o'clock) were about to take their meal called tea.

That little Betsy who looks so small is nearly ten years old: and has been a mother ever since the age of about five. I mean to say, that her own mother having to go out upon her charing operations, Betsy assumes command of the room during her parent's absence: has nursed her sisters from babyhood up to the present time: keeps order over them, and the house clean as you see it: and goes out occasionally and transacts the family purchases of bread, moist sugar, and mother's tea. They dine upon bread, tea and breakfast upon bread when they have it, or go to bed without a morsel. Their holiday is Sunday, which they spend at Church and Sunday-school. The younger children scarcely ever go out save on that day, but sit sometimes in the sun, which comes in pretty pleasantly: sometimes blue in the cold, for they very seldom see a fire except to heat irons by, when mother has a job of linen to get up. Father was a journeyman book-binder, who died four years ago, and is buried among thousands and thousands of the nameless dead who lie crowding the black churchyard of St. Timothy's parish.

The Curate evidently took especial pride in Victoria, the youngest of these three children of the charwoman, and caused Betsy to fetch a book which lay at the window, and bade her read. It was a Missionary Register which the Curate opened haphazard, and this baby began to read out in an exceedingly clear and resolute voice about—

"The island of Raritongo is the least frequented of all the Caribbean Archipelago. Wankyfungo is at four leagues S. E. by E., and the peak of the crater of Shuagnahua is distinctly visible. The *Irascible* entered Raritongo Bay on the evening of Thursday 29th, and the next day the Rev. Mr. Flethers, Mrs. Flethers, and their nine children, and Shang-

POOKY, the native converted at Cacabawgo, landed and took up their residence at the house of RATATATUA, the Principal Chief, who entertained us with yams and a pig," &c., &c., &c.

"Raritongo, Wankyfungo, Archipelago." I protest this little woman read off each of these long words with an ease which perfectly astonished me. Many a lieutenant in HER MAJESTY's Heavies would be puzzled with words of half the length. WHITESTOCK, by way of reward for her scholarship, gave her another pat on the head; having received which present with a curtsey, she went and put the book back into the window, and clambering back into the chair, resumed the hemming of the blue duster.

I suppóse it was the smallness of these people, as well as their singular, neat, and tidy behaviour, which interested me so. Here were three creatures not so high as the table, with all the labours, duties, and cares of life upon their little shoulders, working and doing their duty like the biggest of my readers; regular, laborious, cheerful,—content with small pittances, practising a hundred virtues of thrift and order.

ELIZABETH, at ten years of age, might walk out of this house and take the command of a small establishment. She can wash, get up linen, cook, make purchases, and buy bargains. If I were ten years old and three feet in height, I would marry her, and we would go and live in a cupboard, and share the little half-pint pot for dinner. 'MELIA, eight years of age, though inferior in accomplishments to her sister, is her equal in size, and can wash, scrub, hem, go errands, put her hand to the dinner, and make herself generally useful. In a word, she is fit to be a little housemaid, and to make everything but the beds, which she cannot as yet reach up to. As for VICTORIA's qualifications, they have been mentioned before. I wonder whether the PRINCESS ALICE can read off "Raritongo," &c., as glibly as this surprising little animal.

I asked the Curate's permission to make these young ladies a present, and accordingly produced the sum of sixpence to be divided amongst the three. "What will you do with it?" I said, laying down the coin.

They answered, all three at once, and in a little chorus, "We'll give it to mother." This verdict caused the disbursement of another sixpence, and it was explained to them that the sum was for their own private pleasures, and each was called upon to declare what she would purchase.

ELIZABETH says, "I would like twopenn'orth of meat, if you please, Sir."

'MELIA: "Ha'porth of treacle, three-farthings'-worth of milk, and the same of fresh bread."

VICTORIA, speaking very quick, and gasping in an

agitated manner. "Ha'pny—aha—orange, and ha'-pny—aha—apple, and ha'pny—aha—treacle, and—and—" here her imagination failed her. She did not know what to do with the rest of the money.

At this 'MELIA actually interposed, "Suppose she and VICTORIA subscribed a farthing apiece out of their money, so that BETSY might have a quarter of a pound of meat?" She added that her sister wanted it, and that it would do her good. Upon my word, she made the proposals, and the calculations, in an instant, and all of her own accord. And before we left them, BETSY had put on the queerest little black shawl and bonnet, and had a mug and a basket ready to receive the purchases in question.

Sedan Court has a particularly friendly look to me since that day. Peace be with you, O thrifty, kindly, simple, loving little maidens! May their voyage in life prosper! Think of the great journey before them, and the little cock-boat manned by babies, venturing over the great stormy ocean. SPEC.

II.

FOLLOWING the steps of little BETSY with her mug and basket, as she goes pattering down the street, we watch her into a grocer's shop, where a startling placard with "DOWN AGAIN!" written on it, announces that the Sugar Market is still in a depressed condition—and where she no doubt negotiates the purchase of a certain quantity of molasses. A little further on, in Lawfeldt Street, is MR. FILCH's fine silversmith's shop, where a man may stand for a half hour, and gaze with ravishment at the beautiful gilt cups and tankards, the stunning waistcoat-chains, the little white cushions laid out with delightfnl diamond pins, gold horse-shoes and splinter-bars, pearl owls, turquoise lizards and dragons, enamelled monkeys, and all sorts of agreeable monsters for your neckcloth. If I live to be a hundred, or if the girl of my heart were waiting for me at the corner of the street, I never could pass MR. FILCH's shop without having a couple of minutes' good stare at the window. I like to fancy myself dressed up in some of the jewellery. "SPEC, you rogue," I say, "suppose you were to get leave to wear three or four of those rings on your fingers; to stick that opal, round which twists a brilliant serpent, with a ruby head into your blue satin neckcloth; and to sport that gold jack-chain on your waistcoat. You might walk in the Park with that black whalebone prize-riding-whip, which has a head of the size of a snuff-box, surmounted with a silver jockey on a silver race-horse; and what a sensation you would create, if you took that large ram's horn with the Cairngorm top out of your pocket, and offered a pinch of rappee to the company round!" A little attorney's clerk is staring in at the window, in whose mind very similar ideas are passing. What would he not give to wear that gold pin next Sunday in his blue hunting neckcloth? The ball of it is almost as big as those which are painted over the side door of MR. FILCH's shop, which is down that passage which leads into Trotter's Court.

I have dined at a house where the silver dishes and covers came from FILCH's, let out to their owner by MR. FILCH for the day, and in charge of the grave looking man whom I mistook for the butler. Butlers and ladies' maids innumerable have audiences of MR. FILCH in his back parlour. There are suits of jewels which he and his shop have known for a half century past, so often have they been pawned to him. When we read in the *Court Journal* of LADY FITZBALL's head-dress of lappets and superb diamonds, it is because the jewels get a day rule from FILCH's, and come back to his iron box as soon as the drawing-room is over. These jewels become historical among pawnbrokers. It was here that LADY PRIGSBY brought her diamonds one evening of last year, and desired hurriedly to raise two thousand pounds upon them, when FILCH respectfully pointed out to her Ladyship, that she had pawned the stones already to his comrade, MR. TUBAL, of Charing Cross. And, taking his hat, and putting the case under his arm, he went with her Ladyship to the hack-cab in which she had driven to Lawfeldt Street, entered the vehicle with her, and they drove in silence to the back entrance of her mansion in Monmouth Square, where Mr. Tubal's young man was still seated in the hall, waiting until her Ladyship should be undressed.

We walked round the splendid shining shop and down the passage, which would be dark but that the gas-lit door is always swinging to and fro, as the people who come to pawn go in and out. You may be sure there is a gin-shop handy to all pawnbrokers.

A lean man in a dingy dress is walking lazily up and down the flags of Trotter's Court. His ragged trowsers trail in the slimy mud there. The doors of the pawnbroker's, and of the gin-shop on the other side, are banging to and fro: a little girl comes out of the former, with a tattered old handkerchief, and goes up and gives something to the dingy man. It is ninepence, just raised on his waistcoat. The man bids the child to "cut away home," and when she is clear out of the court, he looks at us with a lurking scowl and walks into the gin-shop doors, which swing always opposite the pawnbroker's shop.

Why should he have sent the waistcoat wrapped in that ragged old cloth? Why should he have sent the child into the pawnbroker's box, and not have gone himself? He did not choose to let her see him go into the gin-shop—why drive her in at the opposite door? The child knows well enough whither he is gone. She might as well have carried an old waistcoat in her hand through the street as a ragged napkin. A sort of vanity, you see, drapes itself in that dirty rag; or is it a kind of debauched shame, which does not like to go naked? The fancy can follow the poor girl up the black alley, up the black stairs, into the bare room, where mother and children are starving, while the lazy ragamuffin, the family bully, is gone into the gin-shop to "try our celebrated Cream of the Valley," as the bill in red letters bids him.

"I waited in this court the other day," WHITESTOCK said, "just like that man, while a friend of mine went in to take her husband's tools out of pawn —an honest man—a journeyman shoemaker, who lives hard by." And we went to call on the journeyman shoemaker—Randle's Buildings—two-pair back —over a blacking manufactory. The blacking was made by one manufactor, who stood before a tub stirring up his produce, a good deal of which—and nothing else—was on the floor. We passed through this emporium, which abutted on a dank, steaming little court, and up the narrow stair to the two-pair back.

The shoemaker was at work with his recovered tools, and his wife was making woman's shoes (an inferior branch of the business) by him. A shrivelled child was lying on the bed in the corner of the room. There was no bedstead, and indeed scarcely any furniture, save the little table on which lay his tools and shoes—a fair-haired, lank, handsome young man with a wife who may have been pretty once, in better times, and before starvation pulled her down. She had but one thin gown; it clung to a frightfully emaciated little body.

Their story was the old one. The man had been in good work, and had the fever. The clothes had been pawned, the furniture and bedstead had been sold, and they slept on the mattress; the mattress went, and they slept on the floor; the tools went, and the end of all things seemed at hand, when the gracious apparition of the Curate, with his umbrella, came and cheered those stricken-down poor folks.

The journeyman shoemaker must have been astonished at such a sight. He is not, or was not a church-goer. He is a man of "advanced" opinions; believing that priests are hypocrites, and that clergymen in general drive about in coaches-and-four, and eat a tithe-pig a day. This proud priest got MR. CRISPIN a bed to lie upon, and some soup to eat; and (being the treasurer of certain good folks of his parish, whose charities he administers) as soon as the man was strong enough to work, the curate lent him money wherewith to redeem his tools, and which our friend is paying back by instalments at this day. And any man who has seen these two honest men talking together, would have said the shoemaker was the haughtiest of the two.

We paid one more morning visit. This was with an order for work to a tailor of reduced circumstances and enlarged family. He had been a master, and was now forced to take work by the job. He who had commanded many men, was now fallen down to the ranks again. His wife told us all about his misfortunes. She is evidently very proud of them. "He failed for seven thousand pounds," the poor woman said, three or four times during the course of our visit. It gave her husband a sort of dignity to have been trusted for so much money.

The Curate must have heard that story many times, to which he now listened with great patience in the tailor's house—a large, clean, dreary, faint-looking room, smelling of poverty. Two little stunted, yellow-headed children, with lean pale faces and large protruding eyes, were at the window staring with all their might at Guy Fawkes, who was passing in the street, and making a great clattering and shouting outside, while the luckless tailor's wife was prating within about her husband's bygone riches. I shall not in a hurry forget the picture. The empty room in a dreary back-ground; the tailor's wife in brown, stalking up and down the planks, talking endlessly; the solemn children staring out of the window as the sunshine fell on their faces, and honest WHITESTOCK seated, listening, with the tails of his coat through the chair.

His business over with the tailor, we start again. FRANK WHITESTOCK trips through alley after alley, never getting any mud on his boots, somehow, and his white neckcloth making a wonderful shine in those shady places. He has all sorts of acquaintance, chiefly amongst the extreme youth, assembled at the doors or about the gutters. There was one small person occupied in emptying one of these rivulets with an oyster shell, for the purpose, apparently, of making an artificial lake in a hole hard by, whose solitary gravity and business struck me much, while the Curate was very deep in conversation with a small-coalman. A half-dozen of her comrades were congregated round a scraper and on a grating hard by, playing with a mangy little puppy, the property of the Curate's friend.

I know it is wrong to give large sums of money away promiscuously, but I could not help dropping a penny into the child's oyster-shell, as she came forward holding it before her like a tray. At first her expression was one rather of wonder than of pleasure at this influx of capital, and were certainly quite worth the small charge of one penny, at which it was purchased.

For a moment she did not seem to know what steps to take; but, having communed in her own mind, she presently resolved to turn them towards a neighbouring apple-stall, in the direction of which she went without a single word of compliment passing between us. Now, the children round the scraper were witnesses to the transaction. "He's give her a penny," one remarked to another, with hopes miserably disappointed that they might come in for a similar present.

She walked on to the apple stall meanwhile, holding her penny behind her. And what did the other little ones do? They put down the puppy as if it had been so much dross. And one after another they followed the penny-piece to the apple-stall.

SPEC.

A DINNER IN THE CITY.

I.

OUT of a mere love of variety and contrast, I think we cannot do better, after leaving the wretched WHITESTOCK among his starving parishioners, than transport ourselves to the City, where we are invited to dine with the Worshipful Company of Bellows-Menders, at their splendid Hall in Marrow-pudding Lane.

Next to eating good dinners, a healthy man with a benevolent turn of mind must like, I think, to read about them. When I was a boy, I had by heart the Barmecides feast in the *Arabian Nights;* and the culinary passages in SCOTT'S novels (in which works there is a deal of good eating) always were my favourites. The Homeric poems are full, as everybody knows, of roast and boiled: and every year I look forward with pleasure to the newspapers of the 10th of November, for the *menu* of the Lord Mayor's feast, which is sure to appear in those journals. What student of history is there who does not remember the City dinner given to the Allied Sovereigns in 1814? It is good even now, and to read it ought to make a man hungry, had he had five meals that day. In a word, I had long, long yearned in my secret heart to be present at a City festival. The last year's papers had a bill of fare commencing with "four hundred tureens of turtle, each containing five pints;" and concluding with the pineapples and ices of the dessert. "Fancy two thousand pints of turtle, my love," I have often said to MRS. SPEC, "in a vast silver tank, smoking fragrantly, with lovely green islands of calipash and calipee floating about—why, my dear, if it had been invented in the time of VITELLIUS he would have bathed in it!"

"He would have been a nasty wretch," MRS. SPEC said, who thinks that cold mutton is the most wholesome food of man. However, when she heard what great company was to be present at the dinner, the Ministers of State, the Foreign Ambassadors, some of the bench of Bishops, no doubt the Judges, and a great portion of the Nobility, she was pleased at the card which was sent to her husband, and made a neat tie to my white neckcloth before I set off on the festive journey. She warned me to be very cautious, and obstinately refused to allow me the CHUBB door-key.

The very card of invitation is a curiosity. It is almost as big as a tea-tray. It gives one ideas of a vast, enormous hospitality. GOG and MAGOG in livery might leave it at your door. If a man is to eat up to that card, Heaven help us, I thought; the Doctor must be called in. Indeed, it was a Doctor who procured me the placard of invitation. Like all medical men who have published a book upon diet, PILLKINGTON is a great gourmand, and he made a great favour of procuring the ticket for me from his brother of the Stock Exchange, who is a Citizen and a Bellows-Mender in his corporate capacity.

We drove in PILLKINGTON'S Brougham to the place of *mangezvous*, through the streets of the town, in the broad daylight, dressed out in our white waistcoats and ties; making a sensation upon all beholders by the premature splendour of our appearance. There is something grand in that hospitality of the citizens, who not only give you more to eat than other people, but who begin earlier than anybody else. MAJOR BANGLES, CAPTAIN CANTERBURY, and a host of the fashionables of my acquaintance, were taking their morning's ride in the Park as we drove through. You should have seen how they stared at us! It gave me a pleasure to be able to remark mentally, "Look on, gents, we too are sometimes invited to the tables of the great."

We fell in with numbers of carriages as we were approaching citywards, in which reclined gentlemen with white neckcloths—grand equipages of foreign ambassadors, whose uniforms, and stars, and gold-lace glistened within the carriages, while their servants with coloured cockades looked splendid without, careered by the Doctor's Brougham-horse, which was a little fatigued with his professional journeys in the morning. GENERAL SIR ROGER BLUFF, K.C.B., and COLONEL TUCKER, were stepping into a cab at the United Service Club as we passed it. The veterans blazed in scarlet and gold-lace. It seemed strange that men so famous, if they did not mount their chargers to go to dinner, should ride in any vehicle under a coach-and-six; and instead of having a triumphal car to conduct them to the city, should go thither in a rickety cab, driven by a ragged charioteer smoking a doodheen. In Cornhill we fell into a line, and formed a complete regiment of the aristocracy. Crowds were gathered round the steps of the old Hall in Marrow-pudding Lane, and welcomed us nobility and gentry as we stepped out of our equipages at the door. The policemen could hardly restrain the ardour of these low fellows, and their sarcastic cheers were sometimes very unpleasant. There was one rascal who made an observation about the size of my white waistcoat, for which I should have liked to sacrifice him on the spot; but PILLKINGTON hurried me, as the policemen did our little Brougham, to give place to a prodigious fine equipage which followed, with immense grey horses, immense footmen in powder, and driven by a grave coachman in an episcopal wig.

A veteran officer in scarlet, with silver epaulets, and a profuse quantity of bullion and silver lace, descended from this carriage between the two footmen, and nearly upset by his curling sabre, which had twisted itself between his legs, which were cased in duck trowsers very tight, except about the knees (where they bagged quite freely), and with rich long white straps. I thought he must be a great man by the oddness of his uniform.

"Who is the general?" says I, as the old warrior, disentangling himself from his scimetar, entered the outer hall. Is it the MARQUESS OF ANGLESEA, or the RAJAH OF SARAWAK?"

I spoke in utter ignorance, as it appeared. "That! Pooh," says PILLKINGTON; "that is MR. CHAMPIGNON, M.P., of Whitehall Gardens and Fungus Abbey, Citizen and Bellows-Mender. His uniform is that of a Colonel of the Diddlesex Militia." There was no end to similar mistakes on that day. A venerable man with a blue and gold uniform, and a large crimson sword-belt and brass-scabbarded sabre, passed presently, whom I mistook for a foreign ambassador at the least; whereas I found out that he was only a Billingsgate Commissioner—and a little fellow in a blue livery, which fitted him so badly that I thought he must be one of the hired waiters of the Company, who had been put into a coat that didn't belong to him, turned out to be a real right honourable gent, who had been a minister once.

I was conducted up-stairs by my friend to the gorgeous drawing-room, where the company assembled, and where there was a picture of GEORGE IV. I cannot make out what public companies can want with a picture of GEORGE IV. A fellow, with a gold chain, and in a black suit, such as the lamented MR. COOPER wears preparatory to execution in the last act of *George Barnwell*, bawled out our names as we entered the apartment. "If my ELIZA could hear that gentleman," thought I, "roaring out the name of 'MR. SPEC!' in the presence of at least two hundred Earls, Prelates, Judges, and distinguished characters!" It made little impression upon them, however; and I slunk into the embrasure of a window, and watched the company.

Every man who came into the room was, of course, ushered in with a roar. "His Excellency the Minister of Topinambo!" the usher yelled; and the Minister appeared, bowing, and in tights. "MR. HOGGIN! The RIGHT HONOURABLE THE EARL OF BARE-

ACRES! MR. SNOG! MR. BRADDLE! MR. ALDERMAN MOODLE! MR. JUSTICE BUNKER! LIEUT.-GEN. SIR ROGER BLUFF! COLONEL TUCKER! MR. TIMS!" with the same emphasis and mark of admiration for us all, as it were. The Warden of the Bellows-Menders came forward and made a profusion of bows to the various distinguished guests as they arrived. He, too, was in a court-dress, with a sword and bag. His lady must like so to behold him turning out in arms and ruffles, shaking hands with Ministers, and bowing over his wine-glass to their Excellencies the Foreign Ambassadors.

To be in a room with these great people gave me a thousand sensations of joy. Once, I am positive, the Secretary of the Tape and Sealing-Wax Office looked at me, and turning round to a noble Lord in a red ribbon, evidently asked, "Who is that?" Oh, ELIZA, ELIZA! How I wished you had been there!—or if not there, in the ladies' gallery in the dining-hall, when the music began, and MR. SHADRACH, MR. MESHACH, and little JACK OLDBOY (whom I recollect in the part of *Count Almaviva* any time these forty years), sang *Non nobis Domine.*

But I am advancing matters prematurely. We are not in the grand dining-hall as yet. The crowd grows thicker and thicker, so that you can't see people bow as they enter any more. The usher in the gold chain roars out name ofter name: more ambassadors, more generals, more citizens, capitalists, bankers—among them MR. ROWDY, my banker, from whom I shrank guiltily from private financial reasons—and, last and greatest of all, "THE RIGHT HONOURABLE THE LORD MAYOR!"

That was a shock, such as I felt on landing at Calais for the first time; on first seeing an Eastern bazaar; on first catching a sight of MRS. SPEC; a new sensation, in a word. Till death, I shall remember that surprise. I saw over the heads of the crowd, first a great sword borne up in the air: then a man in a fur cap of the shape of a flower-pot; then I heard the voice shouting the august name—the crowd separated. A handsome man with a chain and gown stood before me. It was he. He? what do I say? It was his Lordship. I cared for nothing till dinner-time after that. SPEC.

II.

THE glorious company of banqueteers were now pretty well all assembled; and I, for my part, attracted by an irresistible fascination, pushed nearer and nearer my LORD MAYOR, and surveyed him, as the Generals, Lords, Ambassadors, Judges, and other bigwigs rallied round him as their centre, and, being introduced to his Lordship and each other, made themselves the most solemn and graceful bows; as if it had been the object of that General's life to meet that Judge; and as if that Secretary of the Tape and Sealing-wax Office, having achieved at length a presentation to the LORD MAYOR, had gained the end of his existence, and might go home, singing a *Nunc Dimittis.* DON GERONIMO DE MULLIGAN Y GUAYABA, Minister of the Republic of Topinambo, (and originally descended from an illustrious Irish ancestor, who hewed out with his pickaxe in the Topinambo mines the steps by which his family have ascended to their present eminence), holding his cocked hat with the yellow cockade close over his embroidered coat-tails, conversed with ALDERMAN CODSHEAD, that celebrated statesman, who was also in tights, with a sword and bag.

Of all the articles of the splendid court-dress of our aristocracy, I think it is those little bags which I admire most. The dear crisp curly little black darlings! They give a gentleman's back an indescribable grace and air of chivalry. They are at once manly, elegant, and useful (being made of sticking-plaster, which can be applied afterwards to heal many a wound of domestic life). They are something extra appended to men, to enable them to appear in the presence of royalty. How vastly the idea of a Court increases in solemnity and grandeur when you think that a man cannot enter it without a tail!

These thoughts passed through my mind, and pleasingly diverted it from all sensations of hunger, while many friends around me were pulling out their watches, looking towards the great dining-room doors, rattling at the lock (the door gasped open once or twice, and the nose of a functionary on the other side peeped in among us and entreated peace), and vowing it was scandalous, monstrous, shameful. If you ask an assembly of Englishmen to a feast, and accident or the cook delays it, they show their gratitude in this way. Before the supper-rooms were thrown open at my friend MRS. PERKINS's ball, I recollect LIVERSAGE at the door, swearing and growling as if he had met with an injury. So I thought the Bellows-Menders' guests seemed heaving into mutiny, when the great doors burst open in a flood of light, and we rushed, a black streaming crowd, into the gorgeous hall of banquet.

Every man sprang for his place with breathless rapidity. We knew where those places were beforehand; for a cunning map had been put into the hands of each of us by an officer of the Company, where every plate of this grand festival was numbered, and each gentleman's place was ticketed off. My wife keeps my card still in her album; and my dear eldest boy (who has a fine genius and appetite) will gaze on it for half an hour at a time, whereas he passes by the copies of verses and the flower-pieces with an entire indifference.

The vast hall flames with gas, and is emblazoned all over with the arms of by-gone Bellows-Menders. August portraits decorate the walls. THE DUKE OF KENT in scarlet, with a crooked sabre, stared me firmly in the face during the whole entertainment. THE DUKE OF CUMBERLAND, in a hussar uniform, was at my back, and I knew was looking down into my plate. The eyes of those gaunt portraits follow you everywhere. The Prince Regent has been mentioned before. He has his place of honour over the Great Bellows-Mender's chair, and surveys the high table, glittering with plate, epergnes, candles, hock-glasses, moulds of blanc-mange stuck over with flowers, gold statues holding up baskets of barley-sugar, and a thousand objects of art. Piles of immense gold cans and salvers rose up in buffets behind this high table; towards which presently, and in a grand procession—the band in the gallery over-head blowing out the Bellows-Menders' march—a score of City tradesmen and their famous guests walked solemnly between our rows of tables.

Grace was said, not by the professional devotees who sang "*Non Nobis*" at the end of the meal, but by a chaplain somewhere in the room, and the turtle began. Armies of waiters came rushing in with tureens of this broth of the City.

There was a gentleman near us—a very lean old Bellows-Mender, indeed, who had three platefuls. His old hands trembled, and his plate quivered with excitement, as he asked again and again. That old man is not destined to eat much more of the green fat of this life. As he took it, he shook all over like the jelly in the dish opposite to him. He gasped out a quick laugh once or twice to his neighbour, when his two or three old tusks showed, still standing up in those jaws which had swallowed such a deal of callipash. He winked at the waiters, knowing them from former banquets.

This banquet, which I am describing at Christmas, took place at the end of May. At that time the vegetables called peas were exceedingly scarce, and cost six-and-twenty shillings a quart.

"There are two hundred quarts of peas," said the old fellow, winking with blood-shot eyes, and a laugh that was perfectly frightful. They were consumed with the fragrant ducks, by those who were inclined; or with the VENISON, which now came in.

That was a great sight. On a centre table in the hall, on which already stood a cold Baron of Beef—a grotesque piece of meat—a dish as big as a dish in a pantomime, with a little Standard of England stuck into the top of it, as if it was round this we were to rally—on this centre table, six men placed as many huge dishes under cover; and at a given signal the master cook and five assistants in white caps and jackets marched rapidly up to the dish covers, which being withdrawn, discovered to our sight six haunches, on which the six carvers, taking out six sharp knives from their girdles, began operating.

It was, I say, like something out of a Gothic romance, or a grotesque fairy pantomime. Feudal barons must have dined so five hundred years ago. One of those knives may have been the identical blade which WALWORTH plunged in JACK CADE's ribs, and which was afterwards caught up into the City Arms, where it blazes. (Not that any man can seriously believe that JACK CADE was hurt by the dig of the jolly old Mayor in the red gown and chain, any more than that Pantaloon is singed by the great poker, which is always forthcoming at the present season.) Here we were practising the noble custom of the good old times, imitating our glorious forefathers, rallying round our old institutions, like true Britons. These very flagons and platters were in the room before us, ten times as big as any we use or want now-a-days. They served us a grace-cup as large as a plate-basket, and at the end they passed us a rose-water dish, into which PEPYS might have dipped his napkin. PEPYS?—what do I say? RICHARD III., Cœur-de-Lion, GUY OF WARWICK, GOG and MAGOG. I don't know how antique the articles are.

Conversation, rapid and befitting the place and

occasion, went on all round. "Waiter, where's the turtle-fins?"—Gobble, gobble. "Hice Punch or My deary, Sir?" "Smelts or salmon, JOWLER, My boy?" "Always take cold beef after turtle."—Hobble, gobble. "These year peas have no taste." Hobble, gobbleobble. "JONES, a glass of 'Ock with you? SMITH, jine us? Waiter, three 'Ocks. S.! mind your manners. There's MRS. S. a-looking at you from the gallery."—Hobble-obbl-gobble-gob-gob-gob. A steam of meats, a flare of candles, a rushing to and fro of waiters, a ceaseless clinking of glass and steel, a dizzy mist of gluttony, out of which I see my old friend of the turtle soup making terrific play among the peas, his knife darting down his throat.

* * * * * * * *

It is all over. We can eat no more. We are full of BACCHUS and fat venison. We lay down our weapons and rest. "Why, in the name of goodness," says I, turning round to PILLKINGTON, who had behaved at dinner like a doctor; "Why—"

But a great rap, tap, tap proclaimed grace, after which the professional gentlemen sang out "*Non Nobis*," and then the dessert and the speeches began; about which we shall speak in the third course of our entertainment.

III.

On the hammer having ceased its tapping, Mr. Chisel, the immortal toast-maker, who presided over the President, roared out to my three professional friends, "*Non nobis;*" and what is called "the business of the evening," commenced.

First, the Warden of the Worshipful Society of the Bellows-Menders proposed "Her Majesty" in a reverential voice. We all stood up respectfully, Chisel yelling out to us to "Charge our glasses." The royal health having been imbibed, the professional gentleman ejaculated a part of the National Anthem; and I do not mean any disrespect to them personally, in mentioning that this eminently religious hymn was performed by Messrs. Shadrach and Meshech, two well-known melodists of the Hebrew persuasion. We clinked our glasses at the conclusion of the poem, making more dents upon the time-worn old board, where many a man present had clinked for George III., clapped for George IV., rapped for William IV., and was rejoiced to bump the bottom of his glass as a token of reverence for our present sovereign.

Here, as in the case of the Hebrew melophonists, I would insinuate no wrong thought. Gentlemen, no doubt, have the loyal emotions which exhibit themselves by clapping glasses on the tables. We do it at home. Let us make no doubt that the bellows-menders, tailors, authors, public characters, judges, aldermen, sheriffs, and what not, shout out a health for the Sovereign every night at their banquets, and that their families fill round and drink the same toast from the bottles of half-guinea Burgundy.

"His Royal Highness Prince Albert, and Albert Prince of Wales, and the rest of the Royal Family" followed, Chisel yelling out the august titles, and all of us banging away with our glasses, as if we were seriously interested in drinking healths to this royal race: as if drinking healths could do anybody any good; as if the imprecations of a company of bellows-menders, aldermen, magistrates, tailors, authors, tradesmen, ambassadors, who did not care a twopenny-piece for all the royal families in Europe, could somehow affect Heaven kindly towards their Royal Highnesses by their tipsy vows, under the presidence of Mr. Chisel.

The Queen Dowager's health was next prayed for by us Bacchanalians, I need not say with what fervency and efficacy. This prayer was no sooner put up by the Chairman, with Chisel as his Boanerges of a Clerk, than the elderly Hebrew gentlemen before mentioned, began striking up a wild patriotic ditty about the "Queen of the Isles, on whose sea-girt shores the bright sun smiles, and the ocean roars;

whose cliffs never knew, since the bright sun rose, but a people true, who scorned all foes. O, a people true, who scorn all wiles, inhabit you, bright Queen of the Isles. Bright Quee—Bright Quee—ee—ee—ee—ee—en awf the Isles!" or words to that effect, which SHADRACH took up and warbled across his glass to MESHECH, which MESHECH trolled away to his brother singer, until the ditty was ended, nobody understanding a word of what it meant; not OLDBOY—not the old or young Israelite minstrel his companion—not we, who were clinking our glasses—not CHISEL, who was urging us and the Chairman on—not the Chairman and the guests in embroidery—not the kind, exalted, and amiable lady whose health we were making believe to drink, certainly, and in order to render whose name welcome to the Powers to whom we recommended her safety, we offered up, through the mouths of three singers, hired for the purpose, a perfectly insane and irrelevant song.

"Why," says I to PILLKINGTON, "the Chairman and the grand guests might just as well get up and dance round the table, or cut off CHISEL's head and pop it into a turtle-soup tureen, or go through any other mad ceremony as the last. Which of us here cares for HER MAJESTY the QUEEN DOWAGER, any more than for a virtuous and eminent lady, whose goodness and private worth appear in all her acts? What the deuce has that absurd song about the Queen of the Isles to do with HER MAJESTY, and how does it set us all stamping with our glasses on the mahogany?" CHISEL bellowed out another toast—"The Army;" and we were silent in admiration, while SIR GEORGE BLUFF, the greatest General present, rose to return thanks.

Our end of the table was far removed from the thick of the affair, and we only heard, as it were, the indistinct cannonading of the General, whose force had just advanced into action. We saw an old gentleman with white whiskers, and a flaring scarlet coat covered with stars and gilding, rise up with a frightened and desperate look, and declare that "this was the proudest—a-hem—moment of his—a-hem—unworthy as he was—a-hem—as a member of the British—a-hem—who had fought under the illustrious DUKE of—a-hem—his joy was to come among the Bellows-Menders—a-hem—and inform the great merchants of the greatest City of the—hum—that a British—a-hem—was always ready to do his—hum. NAPOLEON—Salamanca—a-hem—had witnessed their—hum, haw—and should any other—hum—ho—casion which he deeply deprecated—haw—there were men now around him—a-haw—who, inspired by the Bellows-Menders' Company and the City of London—a-hum—would do their duty as—a-hum—a-haw—a-hah." Immense cheers, yells, hurrays, roars, glass-smackings, and applause followed this harangue, at the end of which the three Israelites, encouraged by CHISEL, began a military cantata—"O the sword and shield—On the battle-field—Are the joys that best we love boys—Where the Grenadiers, with their pikes and spears through the ranks of the foemen shove boys—Where the bold hurray strikes dread dismay in the ranks of the dead and dyin'—and the baynet clanks in the Frenchmen's ranks, as they fly from the British Lion." (I repeat, as before, that I quote from memory.)

Then the Secretary of the Tape and Sealing Wax Office rose to return thanks for the blessings which we begged upon the Ministry. He was, he said, but a humble—the humblest member of that body. The suffrages which that body had received from the nation were gratifying, but the most gratifying testimonial of all, was the approval of the Bellows-Menders' Company. (*Immense applause.*) Yes, among the most enlightened of the mighty corporations of the City, the most enlightened was the Bellows-Menders. Yes, he might say, in consonance with their motto, and in defiance of illiberality, *Afflavet veritas et dissipati sunt.* (*Enormous applause.*) Yes, the thanks and pride that were boiling with emotion in his bosom, trembled to find utterance at his lip. Yes, the proudest moment of his life, the crown of his ambition, the meed of his early hopes and struggles and aspirations, was at that moment won in the approbation of the Bellows-Menders. Yes, his children should know that he too had attended at those great, those noble, those joyous, those ancient festivals, and that he too, the humble individual who from his heart pledged the assembled company in a bumper—that he too was a Bellows-Mender.

SHADRACH, MESHECH and OLDBOY, at this began singing, I don't know for what reason, a rustic madrigal, describing "O the joys of bonny May—bonny May—a–a–ay, when the birds sing on the spray," &c., which never, as I could see, had the least relation to that or any other ministry, but which were, nevertheless, applauded by all present. And then the Judges returned thanks; and the Clergy returned thanks; and the Foreign Ministers had an innings (all interspersed by my friends' indefatigable melodies); and the distinguished foreigners present, especially MR. WASHINGTON JACKSON, were greeted, and that distinguished American rose amidst thunders of applause.

He explained how Broadway and Cornhill were in fact the same. He showed how WASHINGTON was in fact an Englishman, and how FRANKLIN would never have been an American but for his education as a printer in Lincoln's-Inn-Fields. He declared that MILTON was his cousin, LOCKE his ancestor, NEWTON his dearest friend, SHAKSPEARE his grandfather, or more or less—he vowed that he had wept tears of briny anguish on the pedestal of Charing

Cross—kissed with honest fervour the clay of Runnymede—that BEN JONSON and SAMUEL—that POPE and DRYDEN, and DR. WATTS and SWIFT were the darlings of *his* hearth and home, as of ours, and in a speech of about five-and-thirty minutes explained to us a series of complimentary sensations very hard to repeat or to remember.

But I observed that, during his oration, the gentlemen who report for the daily papers, were occupied with their wine instead of their note-books—that the three singers of Israel yawned, and showed many signs of disquiet and inebriety, and that my old friend, who had swallowed the three plates of turtle, was sound asleep.

PILLKINGTON and I quitted the banqueting-hall, and went into the tea-room, were gents were assembled still, drinking slops and eating buttered muffins, until the grease trickled down their faces. Then I resumed the query which I was just about to put, when grace was called and the last chapter ended. "And, gracious goodness!" I said, "what can be the meaning of a ceremony so costly, so uncomfortable, so savoury, so unwholesome as this? Who is called upon to pay two or three guineas for my dinner now, in this blessed year 1847? Who is it that *can* want muffins after such a banquet? Are there no poor? Is there no reason? Is this monstrous belly-worship to exist for ever?"

"SPEC," the Doctor said, "you had best come away. I make no doubt that you for one have had too much." And we went to his Brougham. May nobody have such a headache on this happy New Year as befell the present writer on the morning after the Dinner in the City! SPEC.

A CLUB IN AN UPROAR. (February 1848.)

THE appearance of a London Club at a time of great excitement is well worthy the remark of a traveller in this city. The Megatherium has been in a monstrous state of frenzy during the past days. What a queer book it would be which should chronicle all the stories which have been told, or all the opinions which have been uttered there.

As a Revolution brings out into light of day, and into the streets of the convulsed capital, swarms of people who are invisible but in such times of agitation, and retreat into their obscurity as soon as the earthquake is over, so you may remark in Clubs, that the stirring of any great news brings forth the most wonderful and hitherto unheard of members, of whose faces not the *habitués*, not even the hall-porters, have any knowledge. The excitement over, they vanish, and are seen no more until the next turmoil calls them forth.

During the past week, our beloved Megatherium has been as crowded as they say HER MAJESTY'S Palace of Pimlico at present is, where distressed foreigners, fugitives, and other COBURGS are crowded two or three in a room; and where it has been reported during the whole of the past week that LOUIS-PHILIPPE himself, in disguise, was quartered in the famous garden pavilion, and plates of dinner sent out to him from HER MAJESTY'S table. I had the story from BOWYER of the Megatherium, who had seen and recognised the ex-king as he was looking into the palace garden from a house in Grosvenor Place opposite. We had other wonderful stories too, whereof it is our present purpose to say a word or two.

The Club, in fact, has been in a state of perfect uproar, to the disgust of the coffee-room *habitués*, of the quiet library arm-chair occupiers, and of the newspaper-room students, who could not get their accustomed broad-sheets. Old DOCTOR POKEY (who is in the habit of secreting newspapers about his person, and going off to peruse them in the recondite corners of the building) has been wandering about, in vain endeavouring to seize hold of a few. They say that a *Morning Chronicle* was actually pulled from under his arm during the last week's excitement. The rush for second editions and evening papers is terrific. Members pounce on the news-boys and rob them. Decorum is overcome.

All the decencies of society are forgotten during this excitement. Men speak to each other without being introduced. I saw a man in ill-made trowsers and with strong red whiskers and a strong northern accent, go up to Colonel the HONOURABLE OTTO DILLWATER of the Guards, and make some dreadful remark about LOUIS FEELIP, which caused the Colonel to turn pale with anger. I saw a Bishop, an Under Secretary of State, and GENERAL DE BOOTS, listening with the utmost gravity and eagerness to little BOB NODDY, who pretended to have brought some news from the City, where they say he is a Clerk in a Fire Office.

I saw all sorts of portents and wonders. On the great Saturday night (the 26th ult.) when the news was rifest, and messenger after messenger came rushing in with wild rumours, men were seen up at midnight who were always known to go to bed at ten. A man dined in the Club who is married, and who has never been allowed to eat there for eighteen years. On Sunday, old MR. PUGH himself, who moved that the house should be shut, no papers taken in, and the waiters marched to church under the inspection of the steward, actually came down and was seen reading the *Observer*, so eager was the curiosity which the great events excited.

In the smoking-room of the establishment, where you ordinarily meet a very small and silent party, there was hardly any seeing for the smoke, any sitting for the crowd, or any hearing in consequence of the prodigious bawling and disputing. The men uttered the most furious contradictory statements there. Young BIFFIN was praying that the rascally mob might be cut down to a man; while GULLET was bellowing out that the safety of France required the re-establishment of the guillotine, and that four heads must be had, or that the Revolution was not complete.

In the card-room, on the great night in question, there was only one whist-table, and at that even they were obliged to have a dummy. CAPTAIN TRUMPINGTON could not be brought to play that night; and PAMM himself trumped his partner's lead, and the best heart; such was the agitation which the great European events excited. When DICKY CUFF came in, from HIS EXCELLENCY LORD PILGRIMSTONE'S evening party, a rush was made upon him for news, as if he had come from battle. Even the waiters appeared to be interested, and seemed to try to overhear the conversation.

Every man had his story, and his private information; and several of these tales I took down.

"*Saturday, five o'clock.* JAWKINS has just come from the City. The French ROTHSCHILD has arrived. He escaped in a water-butt as far as Amiens, whence he went on in a coffin. A *fourgon* containing two hundred and twenty-two thousand two hundred sovereigns, and nine-and-fourpence in silver, was upset in the Rue Saint Denis. The coin was picked up, and the whole sum, with the exception of the fourpenny piece, was paid over to the Commissioners at the Hotel de Ville.

" Some say it was a quarter-franc. It was found sticking, afterwards, to the *sabot* of an Auvergnat, and brought in safety to the Provisional Government.

" BLANKLEY comes in. He made his fortune last year by the railroads, has realised, and is in a frantic state of terror. 'The miscreants!' he says. 'The whole population is in arms. They are pouring down to the English coast; the *sans-culottes* will be upon us to-morrow, and we shall have them upon—upon my estate in Sussex, by Jove! COBDEN was in a league with the Revolutionary government, when he said there would be no war—laying a trap to lull us into security, and so give free ingress to the infernal revolutionary villains. There are not a thousand men in the country to resist them, and we shall all be butchered before a week is out—butchered, and our property confiscated. COBDEN ought to be impeached and hanged. LORD JOHN RUSSELL ought to be impeached and hanged. Hopes GUIZOT will be guillotined for not having used cannon, and slaughtered the ruffians before the Revolution came to a head.' N. B. BLANKLEY was a liberal before he made his money, and had a picture of TOM PAINE in his study.

"Towzer arrives. A messenger has just come to the Foreign Office wounded in three places, and in the disguise of a fishwoman. Paris is in flames in twenty-four quarters—the mob and pikemen raging through it. Lamartine has been beheaded. The forts have declared for the King and are bombarding the town. All the English have been massacred.

"Captain Shindy says, 'Nonsense ! no such thing.' A messenger has come to the French Embassy. The King and family are at Versailles. The two Chambers have followed them thither, and Marshal Bugeaud has rallied a hundred and twenty thousand men. The Parisians have three days' warning : and if at the end of that time they do not yield, seven hundred guns will open on the dogs, and the whole *canaille* will be hurled to perdition.

"Pipkinson arrives. The English in Paris are congregated in the Protestant Churches ; a guard is placed over them. It is with the greatest difficulty that the rabble are prevented from massacreing them. Lady Lunchington only escaped by writing 'Veuve d' O' Connell' on her door. It is perfectly certain that Guizot is killed. Lamartine and the rest of the Provisional Government have but a few days to live : the Communists will destroy them infallibly ; and universal blood, terror, and anarchy will prevail over France, over Europe, over the world.

"Bouncer—on the best authority. Thirty thousand French entered Brussels under LAMORICIERE. No harm has been done to Leopold. The united French and Belgian army march on the Rhine on Monday. Rhenish Prussia is declared to form a part of the Republic. A division under GENERAL BEDEAU will enter Savoy, and penetrate into Lombardy. The Pope abdicates his temporal authority. The Russians will cross the Prusian frontier with four hundred thousand men.

"BOWYER has just come from MIVART'S, and says that rooms are taken there for the Pope, who has fled from his dominions, for the COUNTESS OF LANDSFELD, for the KING OF BAVARIA, who is sure to follow immediately, and for all the French Princes, and their suite and families."

It was in this way that Rumour was chattering last week, while the great events were pending. But oh, my friends! wild and strange as these stories were, were they so wonderful as the truth?—as an army of a hundred thousand men subdued by a rising of bare-handed mechanics; as a great monarch, a minister notorious for wisdom, and a great monarchy blown into annihilation by a blast of national breath; as a magnificent dynasty slinking out of existence in a cab; as a gallant prince, with an army at his back, never so much as drawing a sword, but at a summons from a citizen of the National Guard, turning tail and sneaking away; as a poet braving the pikes which had scared away a family of kings and princes, and standing forward wise, brave, sensible and merciful, undismayed on the tottering pinnacle of popular power? Was there ever a day since the beginning of history, where small men were so great, and great ones so little? What satirist could ever have dared to invent such a story as that of the brave and famous race of Orleans flying, with nobody at their backs; of wives and husbands separating, and the deuce take the hindmost; of ULYSSES shaving his whiskers off, and flinging away even his wig? It is the shamefullest chapter in history—a consummation too base for ridicule.

One can't laugh at anything so miserably mean. All the Courts in Europe ought to go into mourning, or wear sackcloth. The catastrophe is too degrading. It sullies the cause of all kings, as the misconduct of a regiment does an army. It tarnishes all crowns. And if it points no other moral, and indicates no future consequences, why, Progress is a mere humbug: Railroads lead to nothing, and Signs point nowhere: and there is no To-morrow for the world.

SPEC.

WAITING AT THE STATION.

We are amongst a number of people waiting for the Blackwall train at the Fenchurch Street Station. Some of us are going a little farther than Blackwall —as far as Gravesend; some of us are going even farther than Gravesend—to Port Philip, in South Australia, leaving behind the *patriæ fines* and the pleasant fields of old England. It is rather a queer sensation to be in the same boat and station with a party that is going upon so prodigious a journey. One speculates about them with more than an ordinary interest, thinking of the difference between your fate and theirs, and that we shall never behold these faces again.

Some eight-and-thirty women are sitting in the large Hall of the station, with bundles, baskets and light baggage, waiting for the steamer, and the orders to embark. A few friends are taking leave of them, bonnets are laid together, and whispering going on. A little crying is taking place;—only a very little crying,—and among those who remain, as it seems to me, not those who are going away. They leave behind them little to weep for; they are going from bitter cold and hunger, constant want and unavailing labour. Why should they be sorry to quit a mother who has been so hard to them as our country has been? How many of these women will ever see the shore again, upon the brink of which they stand, and from which they will depart in a few minutes more? It makes one sad and ashamed too, that they should not be more sorry. But how are you to expect love where you have given such scanty kindness? If you saw your children glad at the thoughts of leaving you, and for ever: would you blame yourselves, or them? It is not that the children are ungrateful, but the home was unhappy, and the parents indifferent or unkind. You are in the wrong under whose government they only had neglect and wretchedness; not they, who can't be called upon to love such an unlovely thing as misery, or to make any other return for neglect but indifference and aversion.

You and I, let us suppose again, are civilised persons. We have been decently educated: and live decently every day, and wear tolerable clothes, and practise cleanliness: and love the arts and graces of life. As we walk down this rank of eight-and-thirty female emigrants, let us fancy that we are at Melbourne, and not in London, and that we have come down from our sheep-walks, or clearings, having heard of the arrival of forty honest, well-recommended young women, and having a natural longing to take a wife home to the bush—which of these would you like? If you were an Australian Sultan, to which of these would you throw the handkerchief? I am afraid not one of them. I fear, in our present mood of mind, we should mount horse and return to the country, preferring a solitude, and to be a bachelor, than to put up with one of these for a companion. There is no girl here to tempt you by her looks; (and, world-wiseacre as you are, it is by these you are principally moved)—there is no pretty, modest, red-cheeked rustic,—no neat, trim, little grisette, such as what we call a gentleman might cast his eyes upon without too much derogating, and might find favour in the eyes of a man about town. No; it is a homely bevy of women with scarcely any beauty amongst them—their clothes are decent, but not the least picturesque—their faces are pale and care-worn for the most part—how, indeed, should it be otherwise, seeing that they have known care and want all their days?—there they sit upon bare benches, with dingy bundles, and great cotton umbrellas—and the truth is, you are not a hardy colonist, a feeder of sheep, a feller of trees, a hunter of kangaroos—but a London man, and my lord the Sultan's cambric handkerchief is scented with Bond Street perfumery—you put it in your pocket, and couldn't give it to any one of these women.

They are not like you, indeed. They have not your tastes and feelings: your education and refinements. They would not understand a hundred things which seem perfectly simple to you. They would shock you a hundred times a day by as many deficiencies of politeness, or by outrages upon the Queen's English—by practices entirely harmless, and yet in your eyes actually worse than crimes—they have large hard hands and clumsy feet. The woman you love must have pretty soft fingers that you may hold in yours: must speak her language properly, and at least when you offer her your heart, must return hers with its *h* in the right place, as she whispers that it is yours, or you will have none of it. If she says, "O Hedward, I ham so unappy to think I shall never beold you agin,"—though her emotion on leaving you might be perfectly tender and genuine, you would be obliged to laugh. If she said, "Hedward, my art is yours for hever and hever" (and anybody heard her), she might as well stab you,—you couldn't accept the most faithful affection offered in such terms—you are a town-bred man, I say, and your handkerchief smells of Bond-Street musk and millefleur. A sun-burnt settler out of the Bush won't feel any of these exquisite tortures, or understand this kind of laughter: or object to Molly because her hands are coarse and her ancles thick: but he will take her back to his farm, where she will nurse his children, bake his dough, milk his cows, and cook his kangaroo for him.

But between you, an educated Londoner, and that woman, is not the union absurd and impossible?

Would it not be unbearable for either? Solitude would be incomparably pleasanter than such a companion.—You might take her with a handsome fortune, perhaps, were you starving; but then it is because you want a house and carriage, let us say, (*your* necessaries of life,) and must have them even if you purchase them with your precious person. You do as much, or your sister does as much, every day. That however is not the point: I am not talking about the meanness to which your worship may be possibly obliged to stoop, in order, as you say, "to keep up your rank in society"—only stating that this immense social difference does exist. You don't like to own it: or don't choose to talk about it, and such things had much better not be spoken about at all. I hear your worship say, there must be differences in rank and so forth! Well! out with it at once, you don't think MOLLY is your equal—nor indeed is she in the possession of many artificial acquirements. She can't make Latin verses, for example, as you used to do at school, she can't speak French and Italian as your wife very likely can, &c.—and in so far she is your inferior, and your amiable lady's.

But what I note, what I marvel at, what I acknowledge, what I am ashamed of, what is contrary to Christian morals, manly modesty and honesty, and to the national well-being, is that there should be that immense social distinction between the well-dressed classes (as, if you will permit me, we will call ourselves) and our brethren and sisters in the fustian jackets and pattens. If you deny it for your part, I say that you are mistaken, and deceive yourself woefully. I say that you have been educated to it through Gothic ages, and have had it handed down to you from your fathers (not that they were anybody in particular, but respectable, well-dressed progenitors, let us say for a generation or two)—from your well-dressed fathers before you. How long ago is it, that our preachers were teaching the poor "to know their station?" that it was the peculiar boast of Englishmen, that any man, the humblest among us, could, by talent, industry, and good luck, hope to take his place in the aristocracy of his country, and that we pointed with pride to Lord This who was the grandson of a barber; and to Earl That, whose father was an apothecary? what a multitude of most respectable folks pride themselves on these things still! The gulf is not impassable, because one man in a million swims over it, and we hail him for his strength and success. He has landed on the happy island. He is one of the aristocracy. Let us clap hands and applaud. There's no country like ours for rational freedom.

If you go up and speak to one of these women, as you do (and very good-naturedly, and you can't help that confounded condescension), she curtsies and holds down her head meekly, and replies with modesty, as becomes her station, to your honour with the clean shirt and the well-made coat. And so she should; what hundreds of thousands of us rich and poor say still. Both believe this to be bounden duty; and that a poor person should naturally bob her head to a rich one physically and morally.

Let us get her last curtsy from her as she stands here upon the English shore. When she gets into the Australian woods her back won't bend except to her labour; or, if it do, from old habit and the reminiscence of the old country, do you suppose her children will be like that timid creature before you? They will know nothing of that Gothic society, with its ranks and hierarchies, its cumbrous ceremonies, its glittering antique paraphernalia, in which we have been educated; in which rich and poor still acquiesce, and which multitudes of both still admire: far removed from these old world traditions, they will be bred up in the midst of plenty, freedom, manly brotherhood. Do you think if your worship's grandson goes into the Australian woods, or meets the grandchild of one of yonder women by the banks of the Warrawarra, the Australian will take a hat off or bob a curtsy to the new comer? He will hold out his hand, and say, "Stranger, come into my house and take a shakedown and have a share of our supper. You come out of the old country, do you?

There was some people were kind to my grandmother there, and sent her out to Melbourne. Times are changed since then—come in and welcome!"

What a confession it is that we have almost all of us been obliged to make! A clever and earnest-minded writer gets a commission from the *Morning Chronicle* newspaper, and reports upon the state of our poor in London; he goes amongst labouring people and poor of all kinds—and brings back what? A picture of human life so wonderful, so awful, so piteous and pathetic, so exciting and terrible, that readers of romances own they never read anything like to it; and that the griefs, struggles, strange adventures here depicted, exceed anything that any of us could imagine. Yes; and these wonders and terrors have been lying by your door and mine ever since we had a door of our own. We had but to go a hundred yards off and see for ourselves, but we never did. Don't we pay poor-rates, and are they not heavy enough in the name of patience? Very true; and we have our own private pensioners, and give away some of our superfluity, very likely. You are not unkind; not ungenerous. But of such wondrous and complicated misery as this you confess you had no idea? No. How should you?—you and I—we are of the upper classes; we have had hitherto no community with the poor. We never speak a word to the servant who waits on us for twenty years; we condescend to employ a tradesman, keeping him at a proper distance, mind—of course, at a proper distance—we laugh at his young men, if they dance, jig, and amuse themselves like their betters, and call them counter-jumpers, snobs, and what not; of his workmen we know nothing, how pitilessly they are ground down, how they live and die, here close by us at the backs of our houses; until some poet like HOOD wakes and sings that dreadful "*Song of the Shirt;*" some prophet like CARLYLE rises up and denounces woe; some clear-sighted, energetic man like the writer of the *Chronicle* travels into the poor man's country for us, and comes back with his tale of terror and wonder.

Awful, awful poor man's country! The bell rings and these eight-and-thirty women bid adieu to it, rescued from it (as a few thousands more will be) by some kind people who are interested in their behalf. In two hours more, the steamer lies alongside the ship *Culloden*, which will bear them to their new home. Here are the berths aft for the unmarried women, the married couples are in the midships, the bachelors in the fore-part of the ship. Above and below decks it swarms and echoes with the bustle of departure. The Emigration Commissioner comes and calls over their names; there are old and young, large families, numbers of children already accustomed to the ship, and looking about with amused unconsciousness. One was born but just now on board; he will not know how to speak English till he is fifteen thousand miles away from home. Some of these kind people whose bounty and benevolence organised the Female Emigration Scheme, are here to give a last word and shake of the hand to their *protégées.* They hang sadly and gratefully round their patrons. One of them, a clergyman, who has devoted himself to this good work, says a few words to them at parting. It is a solemn minute indeed—for those who (with the few thousand who will follow them) are leaving the country and escaping from the question between rich and poor; and what for those who remain? But, at least, those who go will remember that in their misery here they found gentle hearts to love and pity them, and generous hands to give them succour, and will plant in the new country this grateful tradition of the old.—May Heaven's good mercy speed them!

I.

A NIGHT'S PLEASURE.

HAVING made a solemn engagement during the last Midsummer holidays with my young friend AUGUSTUS JONES, that we should go to a Christmas Pantomime together, and being accommodated by the obliging proprietors of Covent Garden Theatre with a private box for last Tuesday, I invited not only him but some other young friends to be present at the entertainment. The two MISS TWIGGS, the charming daughters of the REV. MR. TWIGG, our neighbour; MISS MINNY TWIGG, their youngest sister, eight years of age; and their maternal aunt, MRS. CAPTAIN FLATHER, as the Chaperon of the young ladies, were the four other partakers of this amusement with myself and MR. JONES.

It was agreed that the ladies, who live in Montpellier Square, Brompton, should take up myself and MASTER AUGUSTUS at the Sarcophagus Club, which is on the way to the theatre, and where we two gentlemen dined on the day appointed. Cox's most roomy fly, the mouldy green one, in which he insists on putting the roaring-grey horse, was engaged for the happy evening. Only an intoxicated driver (as Cox's man always is) could ever, I am sure, get that animal into a trot. But the utmost fury of the whip will not drive him into a dangerous pace; and besides, the ladies were protected by THOMAS, MRS. FLATHER's page, a young man with a gold band to his hat, and a large gilt knob on the top, who ensured the safety of the cargo, and really gave the vehicle the dignity of one's own carriage.

The dinner hour at the Sarcophagus being appointed for five o'clock, and a table secured in the strangers' room, Master Jones was good enough to arrive (under the guardianship of the Colonel's footman) about half-an-hour before the appointed time, and the interval was by him partly passed in conversation, but chiefly in looking at a large silver watch which he possesses, and in hoping that we shouldn't be late.

I made every attempt to pacify and amuse my young guest, whose anxiety was not about the dinner but about the play. I tried him with a few questions about Greek and Mathematics—a sort of talk, however, which I was obliged speedily to abandon, for I found he knew a great deal more upon these subjects than I did—(it is disgusting how preternaturally learned the boys of our day are, by the way.) I engaged him to relate anecdotes about his schoolfellows and ushers, which he did, but still in a hurried, agitated, nervous manner—evidently thinking about that sole absorbing subject, the pantomime.

A neat little dinner, served in Batifol's best manner (our *chef* at the Sarcophagus knows when he has to deal with a connoisseur, and would as soon serve me up his own ears as a *réchauffé* dish), made scarcely any impression on young Jones. After a couple of spoonfuls, he pushed away the Palestine soup, and took out his large silver watch—he applied two or three times to the chronometer during the fish period—and it was not until I had him employed upon an omelette, full of apricot jam, that the young gentleman was decently tranquil.

With the last mouthful of the omelette he began to fidget again; and it still wanted a quarter of an hour of six. Nuts, almonds and raisins, figs (the almost never-failing soother of youth), I hoped might keep him quiet, and laid before him all those delicacies. But he beat the devil's tattoo with the nut-crackers, had out the watch time after time, declared that it stopped, and made such a ceaseless kicking on the legs of his chair, that there were moments when I wished he was back in the parlour of MRS. JONES, his Mamma.

I know oldsters who have a savage pleasure in making boys drunk—a horrid thought of this kind may perhaps have crossed my mind. "If I could get him to drink half-a-dozen glasses of that heavy Port, it might soothe him and make him sleep," I may have thought. But he would only take a couple of glasses of wine. He said he didn't like more; that his father did not wish him to take more: and abashed by his frank and honest demeanour, I would not press him, of course, a single moment further, and so was forced to take the bottle to myself, to soothe me instead of my young guest.

He was almost frantic at a quarter to seven, by which time the ladies had agreed to call for us, and for about five minutes was perfectly dangerous. "We shall be late, I know we shall; I said we should! I am sure it's seven, past, and that the box will be taken!" and countless other exclamations of fear and impatience passed through his mind. At length we heard a carriage stop, and a club-servant entering and directing himself towards our table. Young Jones did not want to hear him speak, but cried out,—"Hooray, here they are!" flung his napkin over his head, dashed off his chair, sprang at his hat like a kitten at a ball, and bounced out of the door, crying out, "Come along, Mr. Speck!" whilst the individual addressed much more deliberately followed. "Happy Augustus!" I mentally exclaimed. "O thou brisk and bounding votary of pleasure! When the virile toga has taken the place of the jacket and turned-down collar, that *Columbine*, who will float before you a goddess to-night, will only be a third-rate dancing female, with rouge, and large feet. You will see the ropes by which the genii come down, and the dirty, crumpled knees of the fairies—and you won't be in such a hurry to leave a good bottle of Port as now at the pleasant age of thirteen."—[By the way, boys are made so abominably comfortable and odiously happy, now-a-days, that when I look back to 1802, and my own youth, I get in a rage with the whole race of boys, and feel inclined to flog them all round.] Paying the bill, I say, and making these leisurely observations, I passed under the hall of the Sarcophagus, where THOMAS, the page, touched the gold-knobbed hat respectfully to me, in a manner which I think must have rather surprised old GENERAL GROWLER, who was unrolling himself of his muffetees and wrappers, and issued into the street, where Cox's fly was in waiting: the windows up, and whitened with a slight frost: the silhouettes of the dear beings within dimly visible against the chemist's light opposite the Club; and MASTER AUGUSTUS already kicking his heels on the box, by the side of the inebriated driver.

I caused the youth to descend from that perch, and the door of the fly being opened, thrust him in. MRS. CAPTAIN FLATHER of course occupied the place of honour—an uncommonly capacious woman,—and one of the young ladies made a retreat from the front seat, in order to leave it vacant for myself; but I insisted on not incommoding MRS. CAPTAIN F., and that the two darling children should sit beside her, while I occupied the place of back bodkin between the two MISS TWIGGS.

They were attired in white, covered up with shawls, with bouquets in their laps, and their hair dressed evidently for the occasion: MRS. FLATHER in her red velvet, of course, with her large gilt state turban.

She saw that we were squeezed on our side of the carriage, and made an offer to receive me on hers.

Squeezed? I should think we *were;* but O EMILY, O LOUISA, you mischievous little black-eyed creatures, who would dislike being squeezed by you? I wished it was to York we were going, and not to Covent Garden. How swiftly the moments passed. We were at the play-house in no time: and AUGUSTUS plunged instantly out of the fly over the shins of everybody.

II.

WE took possession of the private box assigned to us: and MRS. FLATHER seated herself in the place of honour—each of the young ladies taking it by turns to occupy the other corner. MISS MINNY and MASTER JONES occupied the middle places; and it was pleasant to watch the young gentleman throughout the performance of the comedy—during which he was never quiet for two minutes—now shifting his chair, now swinging to and fro upon it, now digging his elbows into the capacious sides of MRS. CAPTAIN FLATHER, now beating with his boots against the front of the box, or trampling upon the skirts of MRS. FLATHER'S satin garment.

He occupied himself unceasingly, too, in working up and down MRS. F.'s double-barelled French opera-glass—not a little to the detriment of that instrument and the wrath of the owner; indeed, I have no doubt, that had not MRS. FLATHER reflected that MRS. COLONEL JONES gave some of the most elegant parties in London, to which she was very anxious to be invited, she would have boxed MASTER AUGUSTUS's ears in the presence of the whole audience of Covent Garden.

One of the young ladies was, of course, obliged to remain in the back row with MR. SPEC. We could not see much of the play over MRS. F.'s turban; but I trust that we were not unhappy in our retired position. O MISS EMILY! O MISS LOUISA! there is one who would be happy to sit for a week close by either of you, though it were on one of those abominable little private box chairs. I know, for my part, that every time the box-keeperess popped in her head, and asked if we would take any refreshment, I thought the interruption odious.

Our young ladies, and their stout chaperon and aunt, had come provided with neat little bouquets of flowers, in which they evidently took a considerable pride, and which were laid, on their first entrance, on the ledge in front of our box.

But, presently, on the opposite side of the house MRS. CUTBUSH, of Pocklington Gardens, appeared with her daughters, and bowed in a patronising manner to the ladies of our party, with whom the CUTBUSH family had a slight acquaintance.

Before ten minutes, the bouquets of our party

were whisked away from the ledge of the box. MRS. FLATHER dropped hers to the ground, where MASTER JONES's feet speedily finished it; MISS LOUISA TWIGG let hers fall into her lap and covered it with her pocket-handkerchief. Uneasy signals passed between her and her sister. I could not, at first, understand what event had occurred to make these ladies so unhappy.

At last the secret came out. The MISSES CUTBUSH had bouquets like little haystacks before them. Our small nosegays, which had quite satisfied the girls until now, had become odious in their little jealous eyes; and the CUTBUSHES triumphed over them.

I have joked the ladies subsequently on this adventure; but not one of them will acknowledge the charge against them. It was mere accident that made them drop the flowers—pure accident. *They* jealous of the CUTBUSHES—not they indeed! and, of course, each person on this head is welcome to his own opinion.

How different, meanwhile, was the behaviour of my young friend MASTER JONES, who is not as yet sophisticated by the world. He not only nodded to his father's servant, who had taken a place in the pit, and was to escort his young master home, but he discovered a schoolfellow in the pit likewise. "By Jove, there's SMITH!" he cried out, as if the sight of SMITH was the most extraordinary event in the world.

He pointed out SMITH to all of us. He never ceased nodding, winking, grinning, telegraphing, until he had succeeded in attracting the attention not only of MASTER SMITH, but of the greater part of the house; and whenever anything in the play struck him as worthy of applause, he instantly made signals to SMITH below, and shook his fist at him, as much as to say, "By Jove, old fellow, ain't it good? I say, SMITH, isn't it *prime*, old boy?" He actually made remarks on his fingers to MASTER SMITH during the performance.

I confess he was one of the best parts of the night's entertainment to me. How JONES and SMITH will talk about that play when they meet after holidays! And not only then will they remember it, but all their lives long. Why do you remember that play you saw thirty years ago, and forget the one over which you yawned last week? Ah, my brave little boy, I thought, in my heart; twenty years hence you will recollect this, and have forgotten many a better thing. You will have been in love twice or thrice by that time, and have forgotten it; you will have buried your wife and forgotten her; you will have had ever so many friendships and forgotten them. You and SMITH won't care for each other, very probably; but you'll remember all the actors and the plot of this piece we are seeing.

I protest I have forgotten it myself. In our

back row we could not see or hear much of the performance (and no great loss)—fitful bursts of elocution only occasionally reaching us, in which we could recognise the well-known nasal twang of the excellent MR. STUPOR, who performed the part of the young hero; or the ringing laughter of MRS. BELMORE, who had to giggle through the whole piece.

It was one of MR. BOYSTER'S Comedies of English Life. FRANK NIGHTRAKE (*Stupor*), and his friend, BOB FITZOFFLEY, appeared in the first scene, having a conversation with that impossible Valet of English Comedy, whom any gentleman would turn out of doors before he could get through half a length of the dialogue assigned. I caught only a glimpse of this Act. BOB, like a fashionable young dog of the aristocracy (the character was played by BULGER, a meritorious man, but very stout, and nearly fifty years of age), was dressed in a rhubarb-colored body-coat with brass buttons, a couple of under waistcoats, a blue satin stock with a paste brooch in it, and an eighteenpenny cane, which he never let out of his hand, and with which he poked fun at everybody. FRANK NIGHTRAKE, on the contrary, being at home, was attired in a very close-fitting chintz dressing-gown, lined with glazed red calico, and was seated before a large pewter teapot, at breakfast. And, as your true English Comedy is the representation of Nature, I could not but think how like these figures on the stage, and the dialogue which they used, were to the appearance and talk of English gentlemen of the present day.

The dialogue went on somewhat in the following fashion:—

Bob Fitzoffley (*enters whistling*). The top of the morning to thee, FRANK! What! at breakfast already? At chocolate and the *Morning Post*, like a dowager of sixty? SLANG! (*he pokes the servant with his cane*) What has come to thy master, thou Prince of Valets! thou pattern of Slaveys! thou swiftest of Mercuries! Has the HONOURABLE FRANCIS NIGHTRAKE lost his heart, or his head, or his health?

Frank (*laying down the paper*). BOB, BOB, I have lost all three! I have lost my health, BOB, with thee and thy like, over the Burgundy at the Club; I have lost my head, BOB, with thinking how I shall pay my debts; and I have lost my heart, BOB, oh, to such a creature!

Frank. A VENUS, of course.

Slang. With the presence of JUNO.

Bob. And the modesty of MINERVA.

Frank. And the coldness of DIANA!

Bob. Pish! What a sigh is that about a woman! Thou shalt be ENDYMION, the night-rake of old: and conquer this shy goddess. Hey, SLANG?

Herewith SLANG takes the lead of the conversation, and propounds a plot for running away with the heiress ; and I could not help remarking how like the comedy was to life—how the gentlemen always say "thou," and "prythee," and "go to," and talk about Heathen goddesses, to each other ; how their servants are always their particular intimates ; how, when there is serious love-making between a gentleman and lady, a comic attachment invariably springs up between the valet and waiting-maid of each ; how LADY GRACE GADABOUT, when she calls upon ROSE RINGDOVE to pay a morning visit, appears in a low satin dress, with jewels in her hair ; how SAUCEBOX, her attendant, wears diamond brooches, and rings on all her fingers : while MRS. TALLYHO, on the other hand, transacts all the business of life in a riding-habit, and always points her jokes by a cut of the whip.

This playfulness produced a roar all over the house, whenever it was repeated, and always made our little friends clap their hands and shout in chorus.

Like that *bon-vivant* who envied the beggars staring into the cook-shop windows, and wished he could be hungry, I envied the boys, and wished I could laugh, very much. In the last Act, I remember—for it is now very nearly a week ago—everybody took refuge either in a secret door, or behind a screen or curtain, or under a table, or up a chimney ; and the house roared as each person came out from his place of concealment. And the old fellow in top-boots, joining the hands of the young couple (FITZ-OFFLEY, of course, pairing off with the widow), gave them his blessing, and thirty thousand pounds.

And ah, ye gods! if I wished before that Comedies were like life, how I wished that life was like Comedies! Whereon, the drop fell; and AUGUSTUS, clapping to the opera-glass, jumped up, crying—"Hurray! now for the Pantomime."

III.

THE composer of the Overture of the New Grand Comic Christmas Pantomime, *Harlequin and the Fairy of the Spangled Pocket-handkerchief, or the Prince of the Enchanted Nose*, arrayed in a bran new Christmas suit, with his wristbands and collar turned elegantly over his cuffs and embroidered satin tie, takes a place at his desk, waves his stick, and away the Pantomime Overture begins.

I pity a man who can't appreciate a Pantomime Overture. Children do not like it: they say, "Hang it, I wish the Pantomime would begin:" but for us it is always a pleasant moment of reflection and enjoyment. It is not difficult music to understand, like that of your MENDELSSOHNS and BEETHOVENS, whose symphonies and sonatas MRS. SPEC states must be heard a score of times before you can comprehend them. But of the proper Pantomime-music I am a delighted connoisseur. Perhaps it is because you meet so many old friends in these compositions consorting together in the queerest manner, and occasioning numberless pleasant surprises. Hark! there goes "*Old Dan Tucker*" wandering into the "*Groves of Blarney;*" our friends the "*Scots wha hae wi' Wallace bled*" march rapidly down "*Wapping Old Stairs*," from which the "*Figlia del Reggimento*" comes bounding briskly, when she is met, embraced, and carried off by "*Billy Taylor*," that brisk young fellow.

All this while you are thinking with a faint, sickly kind of hope, that perhaps the Pantomime *may* be a good one; something like *Harlequin and the Golden Orange Tree*, which you recollect in your youth; something like *Fortunio*, that marvellous and delightful piece of buffoonery, which realised the most gorgeous visions of the absurd. You may be happy, perchance: a glimpse of the old days may come back to you. Lives there the man with soul so dead, the being ever so *blasé* and travel-worn, who does not feel some shock and thrill still? Just at that moment when the bell (the dear and familiar bell of your youth) begins to tingle, and the curtain to rise, and the large shoes and ankles, the flesh-coloured leggings, the crumpled knees, the gorgeous robes and masks finally, of the actors ranged on the stage to shout the opening chorus.

All round the house you hear a great gasping a-ha-a from a thousand children's throats. Enjoyment is going to give place to Hope. Desire is about to be realised. O you blind little brats! Clap your hands, and cram over the boxes, and open your eyes with happy wonder! Clap your hands now. In three weeks more, the REVEREND DOCTOR SWISHTAIL expects the return of his young friends to Sugarcane House.

* * * * * * * *

King Beak, Emperor of the Romans, having invited all the neighbouring Princes, Fairies, and Enchanters to the feast at which he celebrated the marriage of his only son, *Prince Aquiline*, unluckily gave the liver-wing of the fowl which he was carving to the Prince's godmother, the *Fairy Bandanna* while he put the gizzard-pinion on the plate of the *Enchanter Gorgibus*, King of the Maraschino Mountains, and father of the *Princess Rosolia*, to whom the Prince was affianced.

The outraged *Gorgibus* rose from table, in a fury, smashed his plate of chicken over the head of *King Beak's* Chamberlain, and wished that *Prince Aquiline's* nose might grow on the instant as long as the sausage before him.

It did so; the screaming Princess rushed away

from her bridegroom, and her father, breaking off the match with the House of *Beak*, ordered his daughter to be carried in his sedan by the two giant-porters *Gor* and *Gogstay*, to his castle in the Juniper Forest, by the side of the bitter waters of the Absinthine Lake, whither, after upsetting the marriage-tables, and flooring *King Beak* in a single combat, he himself repaired.

The latter monarch could not bear to see or even to hear his disfigured son.

When the *Prince Aquiline* blew his unfortunate and monstrous nose, the windows of his father's palace broke; the locks of the doors started; the dishes and glasses of the King's banquet jingled and smashed as they do on board a steamboat in a storm; the liquor turned sour; the Chancellor's wig started off his head, and the Prince's royal father, disgusted with his son's appearance, drove him forth from his palace, and banished him the kingdom.

Life was a burthen to him on account of that nose. He fled from a world in which he was ashamed to show it, and would have preferred a perfect solitude, but that he was obliged to engage one faithful attendant to give him snuff (his only consolation) and to keep his odious nose in order.

But as he was wandering in a lonely forest, entangling his miserable trunk in the thickets, and causing the birds to fly scared from the branches, and the lions, stags, and foxes to sneak away in terror as they heard the tremendous booming which issued from the fated Prince whenever he had occasion to use his pocket-handkerchief, the Fairy of the Bandanna Islands took pity on him, and, descending in her car drawn by doves, gave him a 'kerchief which rendered him invisible whenever he placed it over his monstrous proboscis.

Having occasion to blow his nose (which he was obliged to do pretty frequently, for he had taken cold while lying out among the rocks and morasses in the rainy miserable nights, so that the peasants, when they heard him snoring fitfully, thought that storms were abroad) at the gates of a castle by which he was passing, the door burst open, and the Irish Giant (afterwards Clown, indeed) came out, and wondering looked about, furious to see no one.

The Prince entered into the castle, and whom should he find there but the *Princess Rosolia*, still plunged in despair. Her father snubbed her perpetually. "I wish he would snub me!" exclaimed the Prince, pointing to his own monstrous deformity. In spite of his misfortune, she still remembered her Prince. "Even with his nose," the faithful Princess cried, "I love him more than all the world beside!"

At this declaration of unalterable fidelity, the Prince flung away his handkerchief, and knelt in rapture at the Princess's feet. She was a little scared at first by the hideousness of the distorted being before her—but what will not woman's faith overcome? Hiding her head on his shoulder (and so losing sight of his misfortune), she vowed to love him still (in those broken verses which only Princesses in Pantomimes deliver).

At this instant *King Gorgibus*, the Giants, the King's Household, with clubs and battle-axes, rushed in. Drawing his immense scimetar, and seizing the Prince by his too-prominent feature, he was just on the point of sacrificing him, when—when, I need not say, the *Fairy Bandanna* (Miss Bendigo), in her amaranthine car drawn by Paphian doves, appeared and put a stop to the massacre. *King Gorgibus* became Pantaloon, the two Giants first and second Clowns, and the Prince and Princess (who had been, all the time of the Fairy's speech, and actually while under their father's scimetar, unhooking their dresses) became the most elegant Harlequin and Columbine that I have seen for many a long day. The nose flew up to the ceiling, the music began a jig, and the two Clowns, after saying "How are you?" went and knocked down Pantaloon.

IV.

On the conclusion of the pantomime, the present memorialist had the honour to conduct the ladies under his charge to the portico of the theatre, where the green fly was in waiting to receive them. The driver was not more inebriated than usual; the young page with the gold-knobbed hat was there to protect his mistresses; and though the chaperon of the party certainly invited me to return with them to Brompton and there drink tea, the proposal was made in terms so faint, and the refreshment offered was so moderate, that I declined to journey six miles on a cold night in order to partake of such a meal. The waterman of the coach-stand, who had made himself conspicuous by bawling out for MRS. FLATHER's carriage, was importunate with me to give him sixpence for pushing the ladies into the vehicle. But it was my opinion that MRS. FLATHER ought to settle that demand; and as, while the fellow was urging it, she only pulled up the glass, bidding Cox's man to drive on, I of course did not interfere. In vulgar and immoral language he indicated, as usual, his discontent. I treated the fellow with playful and, I hope, gentlemanlike satire.

MASTER JONES, who would not leave the box in the theatre until the people came to shroud it with brown-hollands, (by the way, to be the last person in a theatre—to put out the last light—and then to find one's way out of the vast, black, lonely place, must require a very courageous heart)—MASTER JONES, I say, had previously taken leave of us, putting his arm under that of his father's footman, who had been in the pit, and who conducted him to Russell Square. I heard Augustus proposing to have oysters as they went home, though he had twice in the course of the performance made excursions to the cake-room of the theatre, where he had partaken of oranges, macaroons, apples, and ginger-beer.

As the altercation between myself and the link-man was going on, young Grigg (brother of Grigg of the Life Guards, himself reading for the Bar) came up, and hooking his arm into mine, desired the man to leave off "chaffing" me; asked him if he would take a bill at three months for the money; told him if he would call at the Horns Tavern, Kennington, next Tuesday week, he would find sixpence there, done up for him in a brown paper parcel; and quite routed my opponent. "I know *you*, Mr. Grigg," said he; "you're a gentleman, *you* are:" and so retired, leaving the victory with me.

Young Mr. Grigg is one of those young bucks about town, who goes every night of his life to two Theatres, to the Casino, to Weippert's balls, to the Café de l'Haymarket, to Bob Slogger's, the boxing-house, to the Harmonic Meetings at the Kidney Cellars, and other places of fashionable resort. He knows everybody at these haunts of pleasure; takes boxes for the actors' benefits; has the word from head-quarters about the *venue* of the fight between

Putney Sambo and the Tutbury Pet; gets up little dinners at their public-houses; shoots pigeons, fights cocks, plays fives, has a boat on the river, and a room at RUMMER's, in Conduit Street, besides his Chambers at the Temple, where his parents, SIR JOHN and LADY GRIGG, of Portman Square, and Grigsby Hall, Yorkshire, believe that he is assiduously occupied in studying the Law. "TOM applies too much," her ladyship says. "His father was obliged to remove him from Cambridge on account of a brain fever brought on by hard reading, and in consequence of the jealousy of some of the collegians; otherwise, I am told, he must have been Senior Wrangler, and seated first of the Tripod."

"I'm going to begin the evening," said this ingenuous young fellow; "I've only been at the Lowther Arcade, WEIPPERT's hop, and the billiard-rooms. I just toddled in for half an hour to see BROOKE in *Othello*, and looked in for a few minutes behind the scenes at the Adelphi. What shall be the next resort of pleasure, SPEC, my elderly juvenile? Shall it be the Sherry-Cobbler-Stall, or the Cave of Harmony? There's some prime glee-singing there."

"What! is the old Cave of Harmony still extant?" I asked. "I have not been there these twenty years." And memory carried me back to the days when LIGHTSIDES, of Corpus, myself, and little OAKS, the Johnian, came up to town in a chaise-and-four, at the long vacation at the end of our freshman's year, ordered turtle and venison for dinner at the Bedford, blubbered over *Black-eyed Susan* at the play, and then finished the evening at that very Harmonic Cave, where the famous English Improvisatore sang with such prodigious talent that we asked him down to stay with us in the country. SPURGIN, and HAWKER, the fellow-commoner of our College, I remember me, were at the Cave too, and BARDOLPH, of Brazennose. Lord, lord, what a battle and struggle and wear and tear of life there has been since then! HAWKER levanted, and SPURGIN is dead these ten years; little OAKS is a whiskered Captain of Heavy Dragoons, who cut down no end of Sikhs at Sobraon; LIGHTSIDES a Tractarian parson, who turns his head and walks another way when we meet; and your humble servant—well, never mind. But in my spirit I saw them—all those blooming and jovial young boys—and LIGHTSIDES, with a cigar in his face, and a bang-up white coat, covered with mother-of-pearl cheese-plates, bellowing out for "First and Second Turn-out," as our yellow post-chaise came rattling up to the Inn door at Ware.

"And so the Cave of Harmony is open," I said, looking at little GRIGG with a sad and tender interest, and feeling that I was about a hundred years old.

"*I believe you, my baw-aw-oy!*" said he, adopting the tone of an exceedingly refined and popular actor, whose choral and comic powers render him a general favourite.

"Does BIVINS keep it?" I asked, in a voice of profound melancholy.

"Hoh! What a flat you are! You might as well ask if MRS. SIDDONS acted *Lady Macbeth* to-night, and if QUEEN ANNE's dead or not. I tell you what, SPEC, my boy—you're getting a regular old flat—fogy, Sir, a positive old fogy. How the deuce do *you* pretend to be a man about town, and not know that BIVINS has left the Cavern? Law bless you! Come in and see: I know the landlord—I'll introduce you to him."

This was an offer which no man could resist; and so GRIGG and I went through the Piazza, and down the steps of that well-remembered place of conviviality. GRIGG knew everybody; wagged his head in at the bar, and called for two glasses of his particular mixture; nodded to the singers; winked at one friend—put his little stick against his nose as a token of recognition to another; and calling the waiter by his Christian name, poked him playfully with the end of his cane, and asked him whether he, GRIGG, should have a lobster kidney, or a mashed oyster and scolloped 'taters, or a poached rabbit, for supper?

The room was full of young rakish-looking lads, with a dubious sprinkling of us middle-aged youth, and stalwart red-faced fellows from the country, with whisky noggins before them, and bent upon seeing life. A grand piano had been introduced into the apartment, which did not exist in the old days: otherwise, all was as of yore—smoke rising from scores of human chimneys, waiters bustling about with cigars and liquors in the intervals of the melody—and the President of the meeting (BIVINS no more) encouraging gents to give their orders.

Just as the music was about to begin, I looked opposite me, and there, by Heavens! sat BARDOLPH, of Brazennose, only a little more purple, and a few shades more dingy than he used to look twenty years ago.

V.

"LOOK at that old Greek in the cloak and fur collar opposite," said my friend MR. GRIGG. "That chap is here every night. They call him LORD FARINTOSH. He has five glasses of whisky-and-water every night—seventeen-hundred-and-twenty-five goes of alcohol in a year; we totted it up one night at the bar. JAMES the waiter is now taking number three to him. He don't count the wine he has had at dinner." Indeed, JAMES the waiter, knowing the gentleman's peculiarities, as soon as he saw MR. BARDOLPH'S glass nearly empty, brought him another noggin and a jug of boiling water without a word.

Memory carried me instantaneously back to the days of my youth. I had the honour of being at school with BARDOLPH before he went to Brazennose; the under boys used to look up at him from afar off, as at a godlike being. He was one of the head boys of the school; a prodigious dandy in pigeon-hole trowsers, ornamented with what they called "tucks" in front. He wore a ring, leaving the little finger, on which he wore the jewel, out of his pocket, in which he carried the rest of his hand. He had whiskers even then; and to this day I cannot understand why he is not seven feet high. When he shouted out "Under boy!" we small ones trembled and came to him. I recollect he called me once from a hundred yards off, and I came up in a tremor. He pointed to the ground.

"Pick up my hockey-stick," he said, pointing towards it with the hand with the ring on! He had dropped the stick. He was too great, wise, and good, to stoop to pick it up himself.

He got the silver medal for Latin Sapphics, in the year POGRAM was gold medallist. When he went up to Oxford, the Head-Master, the Rev. J. FLIBBER, complimented him in a valedictory speech, made him a present of books, and prophesied that he would do great things at the University. He had got a scholarship, and won a prize-poem, which the DOCTOR read out to the sixth form with great emotion. It was on

"The Recollections of Childhood," and the last lines were,—

> "Qualia prospiciens catulus ferit æthera risu,
> Ipsaque trans lunæ cornua vacca salit."

I thought of these things rapidly, gazing on the individual before me. The brilliant young fellow of 1815 (by-the-bye it was the Waterloo year, by which some people may remember it better; but at school we spoke of years, as "POGRAM'S year," "TOKELY'S year," &c.)—there, I say, sat before me the dashing young buck of 1815, a fat, muzzy, red-faced old man, in a battered hat, absorbing whisky-and-water, and half listening to the singing.

A wild, long-haired professional gentleman with a fluty voice, and with his shirt-collar turned down, began to sing as follows:—

"WHEN THE GLOOM IS ON THE GLEN."

"When the moonlight 's on the mountain
And the gloom is on the glen,
At the cross beside the fountain
There is one will meet thee then.
At the cross beside the fountain;
Yes, the cross beside the fountain,
There is one will meet thee then!

[*Down goes half of* MR. BARDOLPH'S *No.* 3 *Whisky during this refrain.*]

"I have braved, since first we met, love,
  Many a danger in my course;
But I never can forget, love,
  That dear fountain, that old cross,
Where, her mantle shrouded o'er her—
  For the winds were chilly then—
First I met my LEONORA,
  When the gloom was on the glen,
    Yes, I met my, &c.

[*Another gulp and almost total disappearance of Whisky-go, No.* 3.]

"Many a clime I've ranged since then, love,
  Many a land I've wandered o'er;
But a valley like that glen, love,
  Half so dear I never sor!
Ne'er saw maiden fairer, coyer,
  Than wert thou, my true love, when
In the gloaming first I saw yer,
  In the gloaming of the glen!"

BARDOLPH, who had not shown the least symptoms of emotion as the gentleman with the fluty voice performed this delectable composition, began to whack, whack, whack on the mahogany with his pewter measure at the conclusion of the song, wishing, perhaps, to show that the noggin was empty; in which manner JAMES, the waiter, interpreted the signal, for he brought MR. BARDOLPH another supply of liquor.

The song, words, and music, composed and dedicated to CHARLES BIVINS, ESQUIRE, by FREDERIC SNAPE, and ornamented with a picture of a young lady, with large eyes and short petticoats, leaning at a stone cross by a fountain, was now handed about the room by a waiter, and any gentleman was at liberty to purchase it for half-a-crown. The man did not offer the song to BARDOLPH; he was too old a hand.

After a pause, the president of the musical gents cried out for silence again, and then stated to the company that MR. HOFF would sing "*The Red Flag*," which announcement was received by the Society with immense applause, and MR. HOFF, a gentleman whom I remember to have seen exceedingly unwell on board a Gravesend steamer, began the following terrific ballad:—

"THE RED FLAG."

"Where the quivering lightning flings
His arrows from out the clouds,
And the howling tempest sings,
And whistles among the shrouds,
'Tis pleasant, 'tis pleasant to ride
Along the foaming brine—
Wilt be the Rover's bride?
Wilt follow him, lady mine?
Hurrah!
For the bonny, bonny brine.

"Amidst the storm and rack,
You shall see our galley pass,
As a serpent, lithe and black,
Glides through the waving grass;
As the vulture, swift and dark,
Down on the ring-dove flies,
You shall see the Rover's bark
Swoop down upon his prize.
Hurrah!
For the bonny, bonny prize.

"Over her sides we dash,
We gallop across her deck—
Ha! there's a ghastly gash
On the merchant-captain's neck!
Well shot, well shot, old NED!
Well struck, well struck, black JAMES!
Our arms are red, and our foes are dead,
And we leave a ship in flames!
Hurrah!
For the bonny, bonny flames!"

Frantic shouts of applause and encore hailed the atrocious sentiments conveyed by MR. HOFF in this ballad, from every body except BARDOLPH, who sat muzzy and unmoved, and only winked to the waiter to bring him some more whisky.

VI.

WHEN the piratical ballad of MR. HOFF was concluded, a simple and quiet-looking young gentleman performed a comic song, in a way which, I must confess, inspired me with the utmost melancholy. Seated at the table along with the other professional gents, this young gentleman was in no wise to be distinguished from any other young man of fashion: he has a thin, handsome, and rather sad countenance; and appears to be a perfectly sober and meritorious young man. But suddenly (and I daresay every night of his life) he pulls a little flexible, grey countryman's hat out of his pocket, and the moment he has put it on, his face assumes an expression of unutterable vacuity and folly, his eyes goggle round savage, and his mouth stretches almost to his ears, and he begins to sing a rustic song.

The battle-song and the sentimental ballad already published are, I trust, sufficiently foolish, and fair specimens of the class of poetry to which they belong; but the folly of the comic country song was so great and matchless, that I am not going to compete for a moment with the author, or to venture to attempt anything like his style of composition. It was something about a man going a coorting MOLLY, and "feayther," and "kyows," and "peegs," and other rustic produce. The idiotic verse was interspersed with spoken passages, of corresponding imbecility. For the time during which MR. GRINSBY performed this piece, he consented to abnegate altogether his claim to be considered as a reasonable being; utterly to debase himself, in order to make the company laugh; and to forget the rank, dignity, and privileges of a man.

His song made me so profoundly wretched that little GRIGG, remarking my depression, declared I was as slow as a Parliamentary train. I was glad they didn't have the song over again. When it was done, MR. GRINSBY put his little grey hat in his pocket, the maniacal grin subsided from his features, and he sate down with his naturally sad and rather handsome young countenance.

O, GRINSBY, thinks I, what a number of people and things in this world do you represent! Though we weary listening to you, we may moralise over you; though you sing a foolish, witless song, you poor, young, melancholy jester, there is some good in it that may be had for the seeking. Perhaps that lad has a family at home dependent on his grinning: I may entertain a reasonable hope that he has despair in his heart; a complete notion of the folly of the business in which he is engaged; a contempt for the fools laughing and guffawing round about at his miserable jokes; and a perfect weariness of mind at their original dulness and continued repetition. What a sinking of spirit must come over that young man, quiet in his chamber or family, orderly and sensible like other mortals, when the thought of tom-fool hour comes across him, and that at a certain time that night, whatever may be his health, or distaste, or mood of mind or body, there he must be, at a table at the Cave of Harmony, uttering insane ballads, with an idiotic grin on his face, and hat on his head.

To suppose that GRINSBY has any personal pleasure in that song, would be to have too low an opinion of human nature: to imagine that the applauses of the multitude of the frequenters of the Cave tickled his vanity, or are bestowed upon him deservedly—would be, I say, to think too hardly of him. Look at him. He sits there quite a quiet, orderly young fellow. Mark with what an abstracted, sad air he joins in the chorus of MR. SNAPE'S second song, "The Minaret's bells o'er the Bosphorus toll," and having applauded his comrade at the end of the song (as I have remarked these poor gentlemen always do), moodily resumes the stump of his cigar.

"I wonder, my dear GRIGG, how many men there are in the City who follow a similar profession to GRINSBY'S. What a number of poor rogues, wits in their circle, or bilious, or in debt, or henpecked, or otherwise miserable in their private circumstances, come grinning out to dinner of a night, and laugh and crack, and let off their good stories like yonder professional funny fellow. Why, I once went into the room of that famous dinner-party conversationalist and wit, HORSELEY COLLARD; and whilst he was in his dressing-room arranging his wig, just looked over the books on the table before his sofa. There were 'BURTON'S Anatomy' for the quotations, three of which he let off that very night; 'SPENCE'S Literary Anecdotes,' of which he fortuitously introduced a couple in the course of the evening; 'BAKER'S Chronicle;' the last new Novel, and a book of Metaphysics, every one of which I heard him quote, besides four stories out of his common-place book, at which I took a peep under the pillow. He was like GRINSBY." Who isn't like GRINSBY in life? thought I to myself, examining that young fellow.

"When BAWLER goes down to the House of Commons from a meeting with his creditors, and, having been a bankrupt a month before, becomes a patriot all of a sudden, and pours you out an intensely interesting speech upon the West Indies, or the Window Tax, he is no better than the poor gin-and-water practitioner yonder, and performs in his Cave, as GRINSBY in his under the Piazza.

"When SERGEANT BLUEBAG fires into a witness, or performs a jocular or a pathetic speech to a jury, in what is he better than GRINSBY, except in so far as the amount of gain goes?—than poor GRINSBY rapping at the table and cutting professional jokes, at half-a-pint-of-whisky fee?

"When TIGHTROPE, the celebrated literary genius, sits down to write and laugh—with the children very likely ill at home—with a strong personal desire to write a tragedy or a sermon, with his wife scolding him, his head racking with pain, his mother-in-law making a noise at his ears, and telling him that he is a heartless and abandoned ruffian, his tailor in the passage, vowing that he will not quit that place until his little bill is settled—when, I say, TIGHTROPE writes off, under the most miserable private circumstances, a brilliant funny article, in how much is he morally superior to my friend GRINSBY? When LORD COLCHICUM stands bowing and smiling before his sovereign, with gout in his toes and grief in his heart; when parsons in the pulpit—when editors at their desks—forget their natural griefs, pleasures, opinions, to go through the business of life, the masquerade of existence, in what are they better than GRINSBY yonder, who has similarly to perform his buffooning?"

As I was continuing in this moral and interrogatory mood—no doubt boring poor little GRIGG, who came to the Cave for pleasure, and not for philosophical discourse—MR. BARDOLPH opposite caught a sight of the present writer through the fumes of the cigars, and came across to our table, holding his fourth glass of toddy in his hand. He held out the other to me: it was hot, and gouty, and not particularly clean.

"Deuced queer place this, hey?" said he, pretending to survey it with the air of a stranger. "I come here every now and then, on my way home to Lincoln's Inn—from—from parties at the other end of the town. It is frequented by a parcel of queer people—low shop-boys and attorneys' clerks; but hang it, Sir, they know a gentleman when they see one, and not one of those fellows would dare to speak to me—no, not one of 'em, by Jove—if I didn't address him first, by Jove! I don't suppose there's a man in this room could construe a page in the commonest Greek book, SPEC. You heard that donkey singing about 'LEONORAR' and 'before her?' How FLIBBER would have given it to us for such rhymes, hey? A parcel of ignoramuses! but hang it, Sir, they *do* know a gentleman!" And here he winked at me with a vinous bloodshot eye, as much as to intimate that he was infinitely superior to every person in the room.

Now this BARDOLPH, having had the ill-luck to get a fellowship, and subsequently a small private fortune, has done nothing since the year 1820 but get drunk and read Greek. He despises every man who does not know that language (so that you and I, my dear Sir, come in for a fair share of his contempt). He can still put a slang song into Greek Iambics, or turn a police report into the language of TACITUS or HERODOTUS; but it is difficult to see what accomplishment beyond this the boozy old mortal possesses. He spends nearly a third part of his life and income at his dinner, or on his whisky at a tavern; more than another third portion is spent in bed. It is past noon before he gets up to breakfast, and to spell over the *Times*, which business of the day being completed, it is time for him to dress and take his walk to the club to dinner. He scorns a man who puts his h's in the wrong place, and spits at a human being who has not had a University education. And yet I am sure that bustling waiter pushing about with a bumper of cigars; that tallow-faced young comic singer; yonder harmless and happy Snobs, enjoying the conviviality of the evening (and all the songs are quite modest now, not like the ribald old ditties which they used to sing in former days), are more useful, more honourable, and more worthy men, than that whiskyfied old scholar who looks down upon them and their like.

He said he would have a sixth glass if we would stop: but we didn't; and he took his sixth glass without us. My melancholy young friend had begun another comic song, and I could bear it no more. The market carts were rattling into Covent Garden; and the illuminated clock marked all sorts of small hours as we concluded this night's pleasure.

GOING TO SEE A MAN HANGED.

JULY, 1840.

X——, who had voted with Mr. Ewart for the abolition of the punishment of death, was anxious to see the effect on the public mind of an execution, and asked me to accompany him to see Courvoisier killed. We had not the advantage of a sheriff's order, like the "six hundred noblemen and gentlemen" who were admitted within the walls of the prison; but determined to mingle with the crowd at the foot of the scaffold, and take up our positions at a very early hour.

As I was to rise at three in the morning, I went to bed at ten, thinking that five hours' sleep would be amply sufficient to brace me against the fatigues of the coming day. But, as might have been expected, the event of the morrow was perpetually before my eyes through the night, and kept them wide open. I heard all the clocks in the neighbourhood chime the hours in succession; a dog from some court hard by kept up a pitiful howling; at one o'clock, a cock set up a feeble, melancholy crowing; shortly after two, the daylight came peeping grey through the window-shutters; and by the time that X—— arrived, in fulfilment of his promise, I had been asleep about half an hour. He, more wise, had not gone to rest at all, but had remained up all night at the Club, along with DASH and two or three more. DASH is one of the most eminent wits in London, and had kept the company merry all night with appropriate jokes about the coming event. It is curious that a murder is a great inspirer of jokes. We all like to laugh and have our fling about it; there is a certain grim pleasure in the circumstance—a perpetual jingling antithesis between life and death, that is sure of its effect.

In mansion or garret, on down or straw, surrounded by weeping friends and solemn oily doctors, or tossing unheeded upon scanty hospital beds, there were many people in this great city to whom that Sunday night was to be the last of any that they should pass on earth here. In the course of half-a-dozen dark, wakeful hours, one had leisure to think of these (and a little, too, of that certain supreme night, that shall come at one time or other, when he who writes shall be stretched upon the last bed, prostrate in the last struggle, taking the last look of dear faces that have cheered us here, and lingering—one moment more—ere we part for the tremendous journey); but, chiefly, I could not help thinking, as each clock sounded, what is *he* doing now?—has *he* heard it in his little room in Newgate yonder? Eleven o'clock. He has been writing until now. The gaoler says he is a pleasant man enough to be with; but he can hold out no longer, and is very weary. "Wake me at four," says he, "for I have still much to put down." From eleven to twelve the gaoler hears how he is grinding his teeth in his sleep. At twelve he is up in his bed, and asks, "Is it the time?" He has plenty more time yet for sleep; and he sleeps, and the bells go on tolling. Seven hours more—five hours more. Many a carriage is clattering through the streets, bringing ladies away from evening parties; many bachelors are reeling home after a jolly night; Covent Garden is alive; and the light coming through the cell-window turns the gaoler's candle pale. Four hours more! "COURVOISIER," says the gaoler, shaking him, "it's four o'clock now, and I've woke you, as you told me; but there's no call for you to *to get up yet.*" The poor wretch leaves his bed, however, and makes his last toilet; and then falls to writing, to tell the world how he did the crime for which he has suffered. This time he will tell the truth, and the whole truth. They bring him his breakfast "from the coffee-shop opposite—tea, coffee, and thin bread and butter." He will take nothing, however, but goes on writing. He has to write to his mother—the pious mother far away in his own country—who reared him and loved him; and even now has sent him her forgiveness and her blessing. He finishes his memorials and letters, and makes his will, disposing of his little miserable property of books and tracts that pious people have furnished him with. "*Ce* 6 *Juillet*, 1840. *François Benjamin Courvoisier vous donne ceci, mon ami, pour souvenir.*" He has a token for his dear friend the gaoler; another for his dear friend the under-sheriff. As the day of the convict's death draws nigh, it is painful to see how he fastens upon every body who approaches him, how pitifully he clings to them and loves them.

While these things are going on within the prison (with which we are made accurately acquainted by the copious chronicles of such events which are published subsequently), X——'s carriage has driven up to the door of my lodgings, and we have partaken of an elegant *disjeune* that has been prepared for the occasion. A cup of coffee at half-past three in the morning is uncommonly pleasant; and X—— enlivens us with the repetition of the jokes that Dash has just been making. Admirable, certainly—they must have had a merry night of it, that's clear; and we stoutly debate whether, when one has to get up so early in the morning, it is best to have an hour or two of sleep, or wait and go to bed afterwards at the end of the day's work. That fowl is extraordinarily tough—the wing, even, is as hard as a board; a slight disappointment, for there is nothing else for breakfast. "Will any gentleman have some sherry and soda-water before he sets out? It clears the brains famously." Thus primed, the party sets out. The coachman has dropped asleep on the box, and wakes up wildly as the hall-door opens. It is just four o'clock. About this very time they are waking up poor—pshaw! who is for a cigar? X—— does not smoke himself; but vows and protests, in the kindest way in the world, that he does not care in the least for the new drab-silk linings of his carriage. Z——, who smokes, mounts however, the box. "DRIVE TO SNOW HILL," says the owner of the chariot. The policemen, who are the only people in the street, and are standing by, look knowing—they know what it means well enough.

How cool and clean the streets look, as the carriage startles the echoes that have been asleep in the corners all night. Somebody has been sweeping the pavements clean in the night-time surely; they would not soil a lady's white satin shoes, they are so dry and neat. There is not a cloud or a breath in the air, except Z——'s cigar, which whiffs off, and soars straight upwards in volumes of white, pure smoke. The trees in the squares look bright and green—as bright as leaves in the country in June.

We who keep late hours don't know the beauty of London air and verdure; in the early morning they are delightful—the most fresh and lively companions possible. But they cannot bear the crowd and the bustle of mid-day. You don't know them then—they are no longer the same things. We have come to Gray's Inn; there is actually dew upon the grass in the gardens; and the windows of the stout old red houses are all in a flame.

As we enter Holborn the town grows more animated; and there are already twice as many people in the streets as you see at mid-day in a German *residenz* or an English provincial town. The gin-shop keepers have many of them taken their shutters down, and many persons are issuing from them pipe in hand. Down they go along the broad bright street, their blue shadows marching *after* them; for they are all bound the same way, and are bent like us upon seeing the hanging.

It is twenty minutes past four as we pass St. Sepulchre's: by this time many hundred people are in the street, and many more are coming up Snow Hill. Before us lies Newgate Prison; but something a great deal more awful to look at, which seizes the eye at once, and makes the heart beat, is

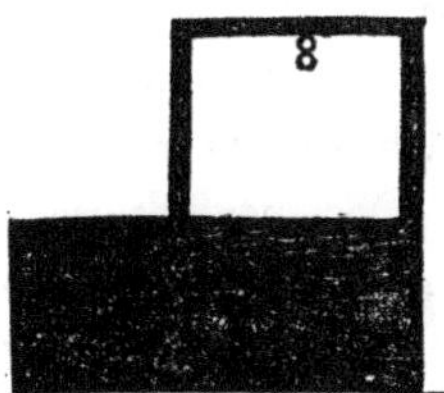

There it stands black and ready, jutting out from a little door in the prison. As you see it, you feel a kind of dumb electric shock, which causes one to start a little, and give a sort of gasp for breath. The shock is over in a second; and presently you examine the object before you with a certain feeling of complacent curiosity. At least, such was the effect that the gallows first produced upon the writer, who is trying to set down all his feelings as they occurred, and not to exaggerate them at all.

After the gallows-shock had subsided, we went down into the crowd, which was very numerous, but not dense as yet. It was evident that the day's *business* had not begun. People sauntered up, and formed groups, and talked; the new comers asking those who seemed *habitués* of the place about former executions; and did the victim hang with his face towards the clock or towards Ludgate Hill? and had he the rope round his neck when he came on the scaffold, or was it put on by Jack Ketch afterwards? and had Lord W—— taken a window, and which was he? I may mention the noble marquess's name, as he was not at the exhibition. A pseudo W—— was pointed out in an opposite window, towards whom all the people in our neighbourhood looked eagerly, and with great respect too. The mob seemed to have no sort of ill-will against him, but sympathy and admiration. This noble lord's personal courage and strength has won the plebs over to him. Perhaps his exploits against policemen have occasioned some of this popularity; for the mob hates them, as children the schoolmaster.

Throughout the whole four hours, however, the mob was extraordinarily gentle and good-humoured. At first we had leisure to talk to the people about us; and I recommend X——'s brother senators of both sides of the house to see more of this same people, and to appreciate them better. Honourable members are battling and struggling in the House; shouting, yelling, crowing, hear-hearing, pooh-pooh-ing, making speeches of three columns, and gaining "great Conservative triumphs," or "signal successes of the Reform cause," as the case may be. Three hundred and ten gentlemen of good fortune, and able for the most part to quote Horace, declare solemnly that unless Sir Robert comes in, the nation is ruined. Three hundred and fifteen on the other side swear their great gods that the safety of the empire depends upon Lord John; and to this end they quote

HORACE too. I declare that I have never been in a great London crowd without thinking of what they call the two "great" parties in England with wonder. For which of the two great leaders do these people care, I pray you? When Lord STANLEY withdrew his Irish bill the other night, were they in transports of joy, like worthy persons who read the *Globe* and the *Chronicle?* or when he beat the ministers, were they wild with delight, like honest gentlemen who read the *Post* and the *Times?* Ask yonder ragged fellow, who has evidently frequented debating-clubs, and speaks with good sense and shrewd good-nature. He cares no more for Lord JOHN than he does for Sir ROBERT; and, with due respect be it said, would mind very little if both of them were ushered out by Mr. Ketch, and took their places under yonder black beam. What are the two great parties to him, and those like him? Sheer wind, hollow humbug, absurd claptraps; a silly mummery of dividing and debating, which does not in the least, however it may turn, affect his condition. It has been so ever since the happy days when Whigs and Tories began; and a pretty pastime no doubt it is for both. August parties, great balances of British freedom: are not the two sides quite as active, and eager, and loud, as at their very birth, and ready to fight for place as stoutly as ever they fought before? But, lo! in the meantime, whilst you are jangling and brawling over the accounts, *Populus*, whose estate you have administered while he was an infant, and could not take care of himself—Populus has been growing and growing, till he is every bit as wise as his guardians. Talk to our ragged friend. He is not so polished, perhaps, as a member of the Oxford and Cambridge Club; he has not been to Eton; and never read HORACE in his life: but he can think just as soundly as the best of you; he can speak quite as strongly in his own rough way; he has been reading all sorts of books of late years, and gathered together no little information. He is as good a man as the common run of us; and there are ten million more men in the country as good as he,—ten million, for whom we, in our infinite superiority, are acting as guardians, and to whom, in our bounty, we give—exactly nothing. Put yourself in their position, worthy sir. You and a hundred others find yourselves in some lone place, where you set up a government. You take a chief, as is natural; he is the cheapest order-keeper in the world. You establish half-a-dozen worthies, whose families you say shall have the privilege to legislate for you for ever; half-a-dozen more, who shall be appointed by a choice of thirty of the rest; and the other sixty, who shall have no choice, vote, place, or privilege, at all. Honourable sir, suppose that you are one of the last sixty: how will you feel, you who have intelligence, passions, honest pride, as well as your neighbour; how will you feel towards your equals, in whose hands lie all the power and all the property of the community? Would you love and honour them, tamely acquiesce in their superiority, see their privileges, and go yourself disregarded without a pang? you are not a man if you would. I am not talking of right or wrong, or debating questions of government. But ask my friend there, with the ragged elbows and no shirt, what he thinks? You have your party, Conservative or Whig, as it may be. You believe that an aristocracy is an institution necessary, beautiful, and virtuous. You are a gentleman, in other words, and stick by your party.

And our friend with the elbows (the crowd is thickening hugely all this time) sticks by *his*. Talk to him of Whig or Tory, he grins at them; of virtual representation, pish! He is a *democrat*, and will stand by his friends, as you by yours; and they are twenty millions, his friends, of whom a vast minority now, a majority a few years hence, will be as good as you. In the meantime we shall continue electing, and debating, and dividing, and having every day new triumphs for the glorious cause of Conservatism, or the glorious cause of Reform, until ——

* * * * *

What is the meaning of this unconscionable republican tirade—*à propos*, of a hanging? Such feelings, I think, must come across any man in a vast multitude like this. What good sense and intelligence have most of the people by whom you are surrounded; how much sound humour does one hear bandied about from one to another? A great number of coarse phrases are used, that would make ladies in drawing-rooms blush; but the morals of the men are good and hearty. A ragamuffin in the crowd (a powdery baker in a white sheep's-wool cap) uses some indecent expression to a woman near; there is an instant cry of shame, which silences the man, and a dozen people are ready to give the woman protection. The crowd has grown very dense by this time, it is about six o'clock, and there is great heaving, and pushing, and swaying to and fro; but round the women the men have formed a circle, and keep them as much as possible out of the rush and trample. In one of the houses near us, a gallery has been formed on the roof. Seats were here let, and a number of persons of various degrees were occupying them. Several tipsy, dissolute-looking young men, of the Dick Swiveller cast, were in this gallery. One was lolling over the sunshiney tiles, with a fierce sodden face, out of which came a pipe, and which was shaded by long matted hair, and a hat cocked very much on one side. This gentleman was one of a party, which had evidently not been to bed on Sunday night, but had passed it in some of those delectable night-houses in the neighbourhood of Covent Garden. The debauch was not over yet, and the women of the party were giggling, drinking, and romping, as is the wont of these delicate creatures; sprawling here and there, and falling upon the knees of one or other of the males. Their scarfs were off their shoulders, and you saw the sun shining down upon the bare white flesh, and the shoulder-points glittering like burning glasses. The people about us were very indignant at some of the proceedings of this debauched crew, and at last raised up such a yell as frightened them into shame, and they were more orderly for the remainder of the day. The windows of the shops opposite began to fill apace, and our before-mentioned friend with ragged elbows pointed out a celebrated fashionable character who occupied one of them; and, to our surprise, knew as much about him as the *Court Journal* or the *Morning Post.* Presently he entertained us with a long and pretty accurate account of the history of Lady ——, and indulged in a judicious criticism upon her last work. I have met with many a country gentleman who had not read half as many books as this honest fellow, this shrewd *prolétaire* in a black shirt. The people about him took up and carried on the conversation very knowingly, and were very little behind him in point of information. It was just as good a company as one meets on common occasions. I was in a genteel crowd in one of the galleries at the queen's coronation; indeed, in point of intelligence, the democrats were quite equal to the aristocrats. How many more such groups were there in this immense multitude of nearly forty thousand, as some say? How many more such throughout the country? I never yet, as I said before, have been in an English mob, without the same feeling for the persons who composed it, and without wonder at the vigorous, orderly good sense, and intelligence of the people.

The character of the crowd was as yet, however, quite festive. Jokes bandying about here and there, and jolly laughs breaking out. Some men were endeavouring to climb up a leaden pipe on one of the houses. The landlord came out and endeavoured, with might and main, to pull them down. Many thousand eyes turned upon this contest immediately. All sorts of voices issued from the crowd and uttered choice expressions of slang. When one of the men was pulled down by the leg, the waves of this black mob-ocean laughed innumerably; when one fellow slipped away, scrambled up the pipe, and made good his lodgement on the shelf, we were all made happy, and encouraged him by loud shouts of admiration. What is there so particularly delightful in the spectacle of a man clambering up a gas-pipe? Why were we kept for a quarter of an hour in deep interest gazing upon this remarkable scene? Indeed it is hard to say: a man does not know what a fool he is until he tries; or, at least, what mean follies will amuse him. The other day I went to Astley's and saw clown come in with a foolscap and pinafore, and six small boys who represented his school-fellows. To them enters schoolmaster; horses clown, and flogs him hugely on the back part of his pinafore. I never read anything in Swift, Boz, Rabelais, Fielding, Paul de Kock, which delighted me so much as this sight, and caused me to laugh so profoundly. And why? What is there so ridiculous in the sight of one miserably rouged man beating another on the breech? Tell us where the fun lies, in this and the before-mentioned episode of the gas-pipe? Vast, indeed, are the capacities and ingenuities of the human soul that can find, in incidents so wonderfully small, means of contemplation and amusement.

Really the time passed away with extraordinary quickness. A thousand things of the sort related here came to amuse us. First, the workmen knocking and hammering at the scaffold, mysterious clattering of blows was heard within it, and a ladder painted black was carried round, and into the interior of the edifice by a small side-door. We all looked at this little ladder and at each other—things began to be very interesting. Soon came a squad of policemen; stalwart, rosy-looking men, saying much for city-feeding; well-dressed, well-limbed, and of admirable good humour. They paced about the open space between the prison and the barriers which kept in the crowd from the scaffold. The front line, as far as I could see, was chiefly occupied by blackguards and boys—professional persons, no doubt, who saluted the policemen on their appearance with a volley of jokes and ribaldry. As far as I could judge from faces, there were more blackguards of sixteen and seventeen, than of any maturer age; stunted, sallow, ill-grown lads, in rugged fustian, scowling about. There were a considerable number of girls, too, of the same age; one that Cruikshank and Boz might have taken as a study for Nancy. The girl was a young thief's mistress evidently; if attacked, ready to reply without a particle of modesty; could give as good ribaldry as she got; made no secret (and there were several inquiries) as to her profession and means of livelihood. But with all this, there was something good about the girl; a sort of devil-may-care candour and simplicity that one could not fail to see. Her answers to some of the coarse questions put to her, were very ready and good-humoured. She had a friend with her of the same age and class, of whom she seemed to be very fond, and who looked up to her for protection. Both of these women had beautiful eyes. Devil-may-care's were extraordinarily bright and blue, an admirably fair complexion, and a large red mouth full of white teeth. *Au reste*, ugly, stunted, thick-limbed, and by no means a beauty. Her friend could not be more than fifteen. They were not in rags, but had greasy cotton shawls, and old, faded, rag-shop bonnets. I was curious to look at them, having, in late fashionable novels, read many accounts of such personages. Bah! what figments these novelists tell us! Boz, who knows life well, knows that his Miss Nancy is the most unreal fantastical personage possible; no more like a thief's mistress, than one of Gessner's shepherdesses resembles a real country wench. He dare not tell the truth concerning such young ladies. They have, no doubt, virtues like other human creatures; nay, their position engenders virtues that are not called into exercise among other women. But on these an honest painter of human nature has no right to dwell; not being able to paint the whole portrait, he has no right to present one or two favourable points as characterising the whole; and therefore, in fact, had better leave the picture alone altogether. The new French literature is essentially false and worthless from this very error—the writers giving us favourable pictures of monsters (and, to say nothing of decency or morality), pictures quite untrue to nature.

But yonder, glittering through the crowd in Newgate Street—see the Sheriffs' carriages are slowly making their way. We have been here three hours!

Is it possible that they can have passed so soon? Close to the barriers where we are, the mob has become so dense that it is with difficulty a man can keep his feet. Each man, however, is very careful in protecting the women, and all are full of jokes and good-humour. The windows of the shops opposite are now pretty nearly filled by the persons who hired them. Many young dandies are there with mustachios and cigars; some quiet, fat, family parties, of simple honest tradesmen and their wives, as we fancy, who are looking on with the greatest imaginable calmness, and sipping their tea. Yonder is the sham Lord W——, who is flinging various articles among the crowd; one of his companions, a tall burly man, with large mustachios, has provided himself with a squirt, and is aspersing the mob with brandy and water. Honest gentleman! high-bred aristocrat! genuine lover of humour and wit! I would walk some miles to see thee on the tread-mill, thee and thy Mohawk crew!

We tried to get up a hiss against these ruffians, but only had a trifling success; the crowd did not seem to think their offence very heinous; and our friend, the philosopher in the ragged elbows, who had remained near us all the time, was not inspired with any such savage disgust at the proceedings of certain notorious young gentlemen, as I must confess fills my own particular bosom. He only said, " So and so is a lord, and they'll let him off," and then discoursed about Lord Ferrers being hanged. The philosopher knew the history pretty well, and so did most of the little knot of persons about him, and it must be a gratifying thing for young gentlemen to find that their actions are made the subject of this kind of conversation.

Scarcely a word had been said about Courvoisier all this time. We were all, as far as I could judge, in just such a frame of mind as men are in when they are squeezing at the pit-door of a play, or pushing for a review or a lord mayor's show. We asked most of the men who were near us, whether they had seen many executions? most of them had, the philosopher especially; whether the sight of them did any good? "For the matter of that, no; people did not care about them at all; nobody ever thought of it after a bit." A countryman, who had left his drove in Smithfield, said the same thing; he had seen a man hanged at York, and spoke of the ceremony with perfect good sense, and in a quiet, sagacious way.

J. S——, the famous wit, now dead, had, I recollect, a good story upon the subject of executing, and of the terror which the punishment inspires. After Thistlewood and his companions were hanged, their heads were taken off, according to the sentence; and the executioner, as he severed each, held it up to the crowd in the proper orthodox way, saying, "Here is the head of a traitor!" At the sight of the first ghastly head the people were struck with terror, and a general expression of disgust and fear broke from them. The second head was looked at also with much interest, but the excitement regarding the third head diminished. When the executioner had come to the last of the heads, he lifted it up, but, by some clumsiness, allowed it to drop. At this the crowd yelled out, "*Ah, Butter-fingers!*"—the excitement had passed entirely away. The punishment had grown to be a joke—Butter-fingers was the word—a pretty commentary, indeed, upon the august nature of public executions, and the awful majesty of the law.

It was past seven now; the quarters rang, and passed away; the crowd began to grow very eager and more quiet, and we turned back every now and then and looked at St. Sepulchre's clock. Half an hour, twenty-five minutes. What is he doing now? He has his irons off by this time. A quarter: he's in the press-room now, no doubt. Now at last we had come to think about the man we were going to see hanged. How slowly the clock crept over the last quarter! Those who were able to turn round and see (for the crowd was now extraordinarily dense), chronicled the time eight minutes, five minutes; at last—ding, dong, dong, dong!—the bell is tolling the chimes of eight.

* * * * * *

Between the writing of this line and the last, the pen has been put down, as the reader may suppose, and the person who is addressing him gone through a pause of no very pleasant thoughts and recollections. The whole of the sickening, ghastly, wicked scene passes before the eyes again; and, indeed, it is an awful one to see, and very hard and painful to describe.

As the clock began to strike, an immense sway and movement swept over the whole of that vast dense crowd. They were all uncovered directly, and a great murmur arose, more awful, *bizarre*, and undescribable than any sound I had ever before heard. Women and children began to shriek horridly. I don't know whether it was the bell I heard; but a dreadful, quick, feverish kind of jangling noise, mingled with the noise of the people, and lasted for about two minutes. The scaffold stood before us, tenantless and black; the black chain was hanging down ready from the beam. Nobody came. "He has been respited," some one said; another said, "He has killed himself in prison."

"Just then, from under the black prison-door, a pale, quiet head peered out. It was shockingly bright and distinct; it rose up directly, and a man in black appeared on the scaffold, and was silently followed by about four more dark figures. The first was a tall, grave man: we all knew who the second man was. "*That's he—that's he!*" you heard the people say, as the devoted man came up.

I have seen a cast of the head since, but, indeed, should never have known it. Courvoisier bore his punishment like a man, and walked very firmly. He was dressed in a new black suit, as it seemed; his shirt was open. His arms were tied in front of him. He opened his hands in a helpless kind of way, and clasped them once or twice together. He turned his head here and there, and looked about him for an instant with a wild, imploring look. His mouth was contracted into a sort of pitiful smile. He went and placed himself at once under the beam, with his face towards St. Sepulchre's. The tall, grave man in black twisted him round swiftly in the other direction, and, drawing from his pocket a nightcap, pulled it tight over the patient's head and face. I am not ashamed to say that I could look no more, but shut my eyes as the last dreadful act was going on, which sent this wretched, guilty soul into the presence of God.

If a public execution is beneficial—and beneficial it is, no doubt, or else the wise laws would not encourage forty thousand people to witness it—the next useful thing must be a full description of such a ceremony, and all its *entourages*, and to this end the above pages are offered to the reader. How does an individual man feel under it? In what way does he observe it,—how does he view all the phenomena connected with it,—what induces him, in the first instance, to go and see it,—and how is he moved by it afterwards? The writer has discarded the magazine "We" altogether, and spoken face to face with the reader, recording every one of the impressions felt by him as honestly as he could.

I must confess, then (for "I" is the shortest word, and the best in this case), that the sight has left on my mind an extraordinary feeling of terror and shame. It seems to me that I have been abetting an act of frightful wickedness and violence, performed by a set of men against one of their fellows; and I pray God that it may soon be out of the power of any man in England to witness such a hideous and degrading sight. Forty thousand persons (say the sheriffs), of all ranks and degrees,—mechanics, gentlemen, pickpockets, members of both houses of parliament, street-walkers, newspaper-writers, gather together before Newgate at a very early hour; the most part of them give up their natural quiet night's rest, in order to partake of this hideous debauchery, which is more exciting than sleep, or than wine, or the last new ballet, or any other amusement they can have. Pickpocket and peer each is tickled by the sight alike, and has that hidden lust after blood which influences our race,—government, a Christian government, gives us a feast every now and then: it agrees, that is to say, a majority in the two Houses agrees, that for certain crimes it is necessary that a man should be hanged by the neck. Government commits the criminal's soul to the mercy of God, stating that here on earth he is to look for no mercy; keeps him for a fortnight to prepare, provides him with a clergyman to settle his religious matters (if there be time enough, but government can't wait); and on a Monday morning, the bell tolling, the clergyman reading out the word of God, "I am the resurrection and the life," "The Lord giveth, and the Lord taketh away,"—on a Monday morning, at eight o'clock, this man is placed under a beam, with a rope connecting it and him; a plank disappears from under him, and those who have paid for good places may see the hands of the government agent, Jack Ketch, coming up from his black hole, and seizing the prisoner's legs, and pulling them, until he is quite dead—strangled.

Many persons, and well-informed newspapers, say that it is mawkish sentiment to talk in this way, morbid humanity, cheap philanthropy, that any man can get up and preach about. There is the *Observer*, for instance, a paper conspicuous for the tremendous sarcasm which distinguishes its articles, and which falls cruelly foul of the *Morning Herald*. "COURVOISIER is dead," says the *Observer;* he "died as he had lived—a villain; a lie was in his mouth. Peace be to his ashes. We war not with the dead." What a magnanimous *Observer!* From this, *Observer* turns to the *Herald*, and says, "*Fiat justitia ruat cœlum.*" So much for the *Herald.*

We quote from memory, and the quotation from the *Observer* possibly is,—*De mortuis nil nisi bonum;* or, *Omne ignotum pro magnifico;* or, *Sero nunquam est ad bonos mores via;* or, *Ingenuas didicisse fideliter artes emollit mores nec sinit esse feros;* all of which pithy Roman apophthegms would apply just as well.

"Peace be to his ashes. He died a villain." This is both benevolence and reason. Did he die a villain? The *Observer* does not want to destroy him body and soul, evidently, from that pious wish that his ashes should be at peace. Is the next Monday but one after the sentence the time necessary for a villain to repent in? May a man not require more leisure—a week more—six months more—before he has been able to make his repentance sure before Him who died for us all?—for all, be it remembered, —not alone for the judge and jury, or for the sheriffs, or for the executioner who is pulling down the legs of the prisoner,—but for him too, murderer and criminal as he is, whom we are killing for his crime. Do we want to kill him body and soul? Heaven forbid! My lord in the black cap specially prays, that

Heaven may have mercy on him; but he must be ready by Monday morning.

Look at the documents which came from the prison of this unhappy Courvoisier during the few days which passed between his trial and execution. Were ever letters more painful to read? At first, his statements are false, contradictory, lying. He has not repented then. His last declaration seems to be honest, as far as the relation of the crime goes. But read the rest of his statement,—the account of his personal history, and the crimes which he committed in his young days,—then, "how the evil thought came to him to put his hand to the work,"—it is evidently the writing of a mad, distracted man. The horrid gallows is perpetually before him; he is wild with dread and remorse. Clergymen are with him ceaselessly; religious tracts are forced into his hands; night and day they ply him with the heinousness of his crime, and exhortations to repentance. Read through that last paper of his; by Heaven, it is pitiful to read it. See the Scripture phrases brought in now and anon; the peculiar terms of tract-phraseology (I do not wish to speak of these often meritorious publications with disrespect); one knows too well how such language is learned,—imitated from the priest at the bedside, eagerly seized and appropriated, and confounded by the poor prisoner.

But murder is such a monstrous crime (this is the great argument),—when a man has killed another, it is natural that he should be killed. Away with your foolish sentimentalists who say no—it is *natural.* That is the word, and a fine philosophical opinion it is—philosophical and Christian. Kill a man, and you must be killed in turn; that is the unavoidable *sequitur*. You may talk to a man for a year upon the subject, and he will always reply to you, It is natural, and therefore it must be done. Blood demands blood.

Does it? The system of compensations might be carried on *ad infinitum*,—an eye for an eye, a tooth for a tooth, as by the old Mosaic law. But (putting the fact out of the question, that we have had this statute repealed by the Highest Authority), why, because you lose your eye, is that of your opponent's to be extracted likewise? Where is the reason for the practice? And yet it is just as natural as the death dictum, founded precisely upon the same show of sense. Knowing, however, that revenge is not only evil, but useless, we have given it up on all minor points. Only to the last we stick firm, contrary though it be to reason and to Christian law.

There is some talk, too, of the terror which the sight of this spectacle inspires, and of this we have endeavoured to give as good a notion as we can in the above pages. I fully confess that I came away down

Snow Hill that morning with a disgust for murder, but it was for *the murder I saw done.* As we made our way through the immense crowd, we came upon two little girls of eleven and twelve years: one of them was crying bitterly, and begged, for Heaven's sake, that some one would lead her from that horrid place. This was done, and the children were carried into a place of safety. We asked the elder girl—a very pretty one—what brought her into such a neighbourhood? The child grinned knowingly, and said, "We've koom to see the mon hanged!" Tender law, that brings out babes upon such errands, and provides them with such gratifying moral spectacles!

This is the 20th of July, and I may be permitted for my part to declare, that, for the last fourteen days, so salutary has the impression of the butchery been upon me, I have had the man's face continually before my eyes; that I can see Mr. Ketch at this moment, with an easy air, taking the rope from his pocket; that I feel myself ashamed and degraded at the brutal curiosity which took me to that brutal sight; and that I pray to Almighty God to cause this disgraceful sin to pass from among us, and to cleanse our land of blood.

THE END.

THACKERAY (the author of "Vanity Fair"), the late ROBERT SOUTHEY, JOHN FORSTER, SIR HUMPHREY DAVY, JOHN WILSON ("Christopher North" of Blackwood), WALTER SAVAGE LANDOR, the Writers for the LONDON TIMES, the leading QUARTERLY REVIEWS, LEIGH HUNT, the late WILLIAM HAZLITT, the authors of the "Rejected Addresses," BARHAM (author of the "Ingoldsby Legends"), SIR FRANCIS HEAD, JAMES MONTGOMERY, &c., &c., comprising generally the most brilliant authors of the Nineteenth Century.

APPLETONS' POPULAR LIBRARY will be printed uniformly in a very elegant and convenient 16mo. form, in volumes of from 250 to 400 pages each, from new type and on superior paper, and will be *bound* in a novel and attractive style for preservation, in fancy cloth, and will be sold at the average price of fifty cents per volume.

The following books, indicating the variety of the series, are preparing for immediate publication; and orders of the Trade are solicited:—

ESSAYS: A SERIES OF PERSONAL AND HISTORICAL SKETCHES FROM THE LONDON TIMES.

LIFE AND MISCELLANIES OF THEODORE HOOK.

JOHN FORSTER'S LIFE OF GOLDSMITH.

THE YELLOWPLUSH PAPERS AND OTHER VOLUMES, BY WILLIAM M. THACKERAY, AUTHOR OF "VANITY FAIR."

JEREMY TAYLOR; A BIOGRAPHY, BY ROBERT ARIS WILLMOTT.

LEIGH HUNT'S BOOK FOR A CORNER.

THE MISCELLANEOUS WRITINGS OF JAMES AND HORACE SMITH, THE AUTHORS OF THE "REJECTED ADDRESSES."

THE INGOLDSBY LEGENDS, BY BARHAM.

LITTLE PEDLINGTON AND THE PEDLINGTONIANS BY JOHN POOLE, AUTHOR OF "PAUL PRY."

&c., &c., &c.

APPLETONS' POPULAR LIBRARY.

THE MAIDEN AND MARRIED LIFE OF MARY POWELL,

AFTERWARDS MISTRESS MILTON.

Price Fifty Cents

"A reproduction "in their manners as they lived" of John Milton and his young bride, of whom the anecdote of their separation and reconciliation is told in Dr. Johnson's biography of the poet. The narrative is in the style of the period as the Diary of Lady Willoughby is written, and is remarkable for its feminine grace and character—and the interest of real life artistically disposed: a book for the selected shelf of the lady's boudoir in its touches of nature and sentiment no less than as a study of one of England's greatest poets "at home."

ENGLISH NOTICES.

"This is a charming book; and whether we regard its subject, cleverness or delicacy of sentiment and expression, it is likely to be a most acceptable present to young or old, be their peculiar taste for religion, morals, poetry, history, or romance."—*Christian Observer.*

"Unquestionably the production of an able hand, and a refined mind. We recommend it to all who love pure, healthy literary fare."—*Church and State Gazette.*

"Full of incident and character, and exceedingly delightful in its happy sketching and freshness of feeling. It is by far the best work of the small and novel class to which it belongs, a mixture of truth and fiction in a form which belongs to the fictitious more than to the substantial contents."—*Nonconformist.*

"The odd history of Milton's first marriage—the desertion of his wife, and her subsequent terror when she heard that he was just the man to put in practice his own opinions respecting divorce—forms one of those chapters, peculiarly open to illustration and fancy."—*Atlas.*

www.ingramcontent.com/pod-product-compliance
Lightning Source LLC
LaVergne TN
LVHW020234110826
845151LV00003B/925

* 9 7 8 1 4 2 5 5 2 9 6 6 6 *